B.F. SKINNER'S
BEHAVIORISM
AN ANALYSIS

ABOUT THE AUTHOR

MARK P. COSGROVE Mark Cosgrove is Associate Professor of Psychology at Taylor University in Upland, Indiana. He obtained his B.A. at Creighton University, and his M.S. and Ph.D. in experimental psychology from Purdue University. He was a visiting Assistant Professor in the Department of Psychology at Purdue in the fall of 1973 before serving as a research associate with Probe Ministries International from 1974 to 1976. He is a member of Sigma Xi, the Midwestern Psychological Association, and the American Scientific Affiliation. Dr. Cosgrove has published frequently in *Vision Research* and in *Perception and Psychophysics*.

B.F. SKINNER'S BEHAVIORISM
AN ANALYSIS

MARK P. COSGROVE

ZONDERVAN
PUBLISHING HOUSE
OF THE ZONDERVAN CORPORATION
GRAND RAPIDS, MICHIGAN 49506

B. F. Skinner's Behaviorism: An Analysis
Copyright © 1982 by The Zondervan Corporation
Grand Rapids, Michigan

Library of Congress Cataloging in Publication Data

Cosgrove, Mark P.
    B. F. Skinner's behaviorism.

    (Rosemead psychology series)
    Bibliography: p.
    Includes index.
    1. Skinner, B. F. (Burrhus Frederic), 1904– . 2. Behaviorism (Psychology)
I. Title. II. Series.

BF199.C67   1982   150.19′434′0924   82-10993
ISBN 0-310-44491-8

Edited by Ben Chapman

Printed in the United States of America

82   83   84   85   86   87   88 — 10   9   8   7   6   5   4   3   2   1

THE ROSEMEAD PSYCHOLOGY SERIES

The Rosemead Psychology Series is a continuing series of studies written for professionals and students in the fields of psychology and theology and in related areas such as pastoral counseling. It seeks to present current thinking on the subject of the integration of psychology and the Christian faith by examining key issues and problems that grow out of the interface of psychology and theology. The data and theories of both theoretical and applied psychology are treated in this series, as well as fundamental theological concepts and issues that bear on psychological research, theory, and practice. These volumes are offered with the hope that they will stimulate further thinking and publication on the integration of psychology and the Christian faith.

Editor

BRUCE NARRAMORE
Dean and Professor of Psychology
Rosemead School of Psychology
Biola University

Consulting Editors

JOHN D. CARTER
Professor of Psychology
Rosemead School
  of Psychology
Biola University

J. ROLAND FLECK
Associate Professor of Psychology
Rosemead School
  of Psychology
Biola University

CONTENTS

THE CHALLENGE

1

What is being abolished is autonomous man — the inner man. . . . His abolition has long been overdue. Autonomous man is a device used to explain what we cannot explain in any other way. He has been constructed from our ignorance. (p. 191)

A scientific view of man offers exciting possibilities. We have not yet seen what man can make of man. (p. 206)

The above words were penned by the distinguished psychologist B. F. Skinner (1971), who is considered by many to be the most important psychologist of this century. He is today's leading spokesman for behaviorism and the champion behind psychological engineering. His operant conditioning theory has produced noticeable changes in American education, counseling, and business management. *Time* magazine (Sept. 20, 1971) called Skinner, "the most influential of living American psychologists, and the most controversial contemporary figure in the science of human behavior, adored as a messiah and abhorred as a menace" (p. 47).

Skinner is a continual focus of debate because he is firmly

9

committed to the propositions that human nature can be completely understood through the methods of natural science; that human behavior is determined by the environment; and that the psychological control of human behavior is the only hope for the immense problems facing mankind in the twentieth century. These ideas, however, cut against the grain of much of the philosophical and theological thought of the last twenty-five hundred years and have caused many to raise cries of alarm or serious philosophical questions about their adequacy. Francis Schaeffer (1972), for example, writes:

> We are on the verge of the largest revolution the world has ever seen—the control and shaping of men through genetic engineering and chemical and psychological conditioning. Will people accept it? I don't think they would accept it if (1) they had not already been taught to accept the presuppositions that lead to it and (2) they were not in such despair. But many have accepted the presuppositions and they are in despair. (pp. 35, 44)

Many others have apprehensively seen in Skinner's work the prophetic shades of *1984, Brave New World,* or *A Clockwork Orange,* with their images of dictatorial controllers with advanced academic degrees in behavioristic psychology (obviously).

Skinner, on the other hand, sees his ideas as the solid product of years of careful scientific research. He feels that his research and writings on behaviorism have sufficiently countered the inept theologies and literatures of freedom and dignity. In his opinion behaviorism is the only area of psychology worth studying today. As he stated in an interview with *Psychology Today* (Hall, 1967):

> I think we have put our finger on something of extraordinary importance here—and when we get the truth out, everything will follow these operant rules which we have seen and are still discovering. With them one cannot make a very serious mistake. And since this is where the future of psychology lies, it's well worth the telling. (p. 71)

Skinner is not far from correct when he assesses the importance of the work he has produced. While he may be extreme in his view that behaviorism contains most of the truth worth telling in psychology, Skinner has had such a great impact on our society that no educated person should be ignorant of his theories.

Skinner began his research in the 1930's studying the conditioning of rats and other animals in highly controlled experimental chambers. Since that time his basic research methods and ideas have been used to speed up animal learning, improve patient behavior in psychiatric wards, cure problems like bed wetting and stuttering, eliminate disruptive or delinquent behaviors, improve human learning ability and speed, develop self-control of unwanted habits, and more. Skinner's inventive flair captured popular attention when he unveiled such behavioristic offerings as teaching machines, pigeons that played ping pong, and scientifically designed baby cribs. His work has also spawned a host of successful graduate students and spurred the proliferation of new journals devoted to behavioristic topics.[1]

It has not been only on the lofty scientific level that Skinner's influence has been felt, but on the popular level as well. Who of us has not heard parents state in Skinner's own language that they hesitated to rush to their crying baby's crib lest they "reinforce" its crying behavior? Everyone who takes an introductory psychology class comes away thinking a little more like a behaviorist. It has become increasingly obvious that Skinner's behaviorism is an important part of the fabric of our thinking and our daily lives. Because of this great influence and the fact that Skinner's behavior control applications are being proposed for the large-scale management of society, it is of utmost importance for us to critically examine and count the cost of the behaviorism we are being sold.

FIVE CHALLENGES There are five aspects of Skinner's behaviorism that challenge traditional ways of looking at life. These areas challenge assumptions of the academic

[1]The following list of journals and their founding dates chronicles the growth of behavioristic research as Skinner's theories became increasingly more accepted by the scientific community. *Journal of the Experimental Analysis of Behavior* (1958); *Behavior Research and Therapy* (1962); *The Journal of Applied Behavior Analysis* (1968); *Behavior Therapy* (1970); *Behavior Therapy and Experimental Psychiatry* (1970); *Journal of Behavior Technology* (1971).

community and society at large and therefore demand our careful examination. This book will attempt to bring these challenges into focus.

The Challenge To Human Dignity

The data and theories of Skinner have been used to challenge the traditional view that human nature is something intangible and free. While Skinner is a descendant of a long line of academic scientists who have challenged such lofty views of man, and while he made his views quite clear in earlier writings, it was not until his *Beyond Freedom and Dignity* filled the book racks in 1971 that his mechanistic views on human nature became widely known and debated. Skinner was of the opinion that, for too long the truth about the control of human nature by environment had been hidden in technical jargon and the data graphs of behavioristic journals. Therefore, in 1971, the challenge was delivered to the public.

The Challenge To Human Freedom

Skinner's challenge to the traditional concept of human free-dom and responsibility deserves careful examination and critique for two reasons. First, since scientists believe less and less in the freedom and dignity of man, their applications and technologies could begin to treat man with less humaneness and dignity. Historically, when a segment of the population has been considered to be less than human technically (e.g., the mentally disturbed, the human fetus, a minority group), that segment has been treated with less humaneness practically.

Second, as the prevailing lofty view of human nature and free-dom declines, even if that view is correct, individuals in society can begin to lose the awareness of their own freedom and the confi-dence in their own ability to resist environmental influences. The concept of self-fulfilling prophecy predicts that if science leads us to believe that everything we do is caused by our genes and our envi-ronments, we will begin to lose the ability to direct our own futures. Our society would become more passive, and educators, therapists, and jurists would be less and less inclined to view individuals as

THE CHALLENGE ■ 13

responsible—even for criminal behaviors. Even if Skinner's theories on determinism are not true, human nature is still in danger of becoming a piece of the environment by default. This is part of what C. S. Lewis (1947) meant when he wrote:

> It is in Man's power to treat himself as a mere 'natural object' and his own judgements of value as raw material for scientific manipulation to alter at will. The objection to his doing so does not lie in the fact that his point of view (like one's first day in a dissecting room) is painful and shocking till we grow used to it. The pain and shock are at most a warning and a symptom. The real objection is that if man chooses to treat himself as raw material, raw material he will be; not raw material to be manipulated, as he fondly imagined by himself, but by mere appetite, that is mere Nature, in the person of his dehumanized Conditioners. (p. 84)

The Challenge To Value

Skinner's behaviorism and its accompanying technology also raise a major challenge in the area of values. There is no doubt that the science of behaviorism has been sufficiently developed to permit its use in individual settings and for small-scale social control. Even this limited usage raises serious questions of values and ethics and the possibility of wide-spread social control raises questions that can challenge the very foundations of the ethical values of our society.

Skinner suggests a general value structure that can guide behavioral technology and ultimately address questions like, What is the optimum in human personality and behavior that these technologies are attempting to produce? What restrictions guide the use of punishment? and Is the group to be valued over the individual? How are we to respond to his proposed directions and does his naturalistic philosophy provide an adequate basis for answering the tough ethical questions science and technology are raising? This challenge is also posed by the other natural and social sciences and it is a crucial one.

The Challenge To Philosophy

A fourth challenge set forth by Skinner is a philosophical one. Skinner claims that when anyone criticizes his views, the argument is not with him, but with well-demonstrated, scientific facts. By suggesting that his critics, with all of their high-sounding philosophical criticism, have failed to understand the science behind his psychological theory, Skinner essentially attempts to wipe out all competing philosophical views. Considering the credibility our culture has given to science, this challenge has been effective for Skinner in some quarters.

To face this challenge Skinner's critics point out that a particular scientific enterprise is only as sound as its philosophical assumptions. They suggest that Skinner is not speaking as much from laboratory data about human nature and human freedom as he is from prior assumptions regarding materialism, empiricism, determinism, and the nature of acceptable data in psychology. Skinner's science needs to be examined in the light of these assumptions to see what in his theory is a product of his science and what is a product of his assumptions.

The Challenge To Human Problems

A final challenge posed by Skinner is his willingness to apply his scientific theory to even very difficult human problems. One cannot listen to or read Skinner without sensing his concern for human beings and the future of the human race. Since he believes the problems of war, pullution, crime, and emotional illness can be solved by his technology, he is challenging all alternative views for social change. Included in this challenge is a questioning of the entire Judeo-Christian view of human nature and the potential for the Gospel of Jesus Christ to change human nature and to heal personal and social problems. In many ways the Christian scientist should be challenged by Skinner's last words in *Beyond Freedom and Dignity*. "A scientific view of man offers exciting possibilities. We have not yet seen what man can make of man" (p. 206).

SKINNER'S "ENVIRONMENTAL HISTORY" Since, for Skinner's behaviorism, the environment is seen as the controller of a person's behavior, it seems appropriate to consider Skinner's environmental

FIGURE 1

"B. F. Skinner" photo courtesy of B. F. Skinner

history with an eye to its "influences" on Skinner. Skinner is one of the more interesting psychologists of our time. It took an unusual individual to sculpt from dull learning theories such things as pigeons that fly missiles and a well-written novel about a behaviorally engineered community. He is also a man who saw fit to live within at least some of his own ideas. His younger daughter spent most of the first thirty months of her life in an air crib, a large box with climate control. He even charts his own productive hours in his office in the same way that he charts the behaviors of his animals!

Skinner was raised in rather ordinary family, academic, and religious surroundings. His Bible training, which he describes as "liberal," did not foster in him a belief in the supernatural. In fact, early in his teens he announced to one of his teachers that he no longer believed in God; he has not regained that belief. How much his atheism affected his later beliefs on reality, man, and ethics is difficult to determine, but that assumption must be recognized as an environmental factor.

Skinner graduated from college with a major in English and what might be called a minor in fun-loving pranks. His literary abilities had been appraised when he was still a senior in college by Robert Frost, who wrote him encouraging comments. After graduation Skinner went to Greenwich Village and spent six months as a writer. He felt he was a failure at writing, because he had nothing to say, and he began to wonder if the literary method was as effective as science in changing things.

Skinner's interest in psychology was strengthened by his reading of Pavlov's *Conditioned Reflexes* (1927), Bertrand Russell's *Philosophy* (1925), which devoted a lot of time to John Watson's behaviorism (1924–25) and Watson's book. After this time period Skinner enrolled in Harvard for graduate study in psychology.

After graduate work under Edwin Boring and postdoctoral research at Harvard, Skinner went to the University of Minnesota. There he taught for the first time, lecturing to large introductory psychology sections. Since he was teaching from material that would later become his first book, *The Behavior of Organisms* (1938), one wonders whether his students were aware that they were hearing a legend-to-be speaking on ideas that were soon to dominate the entire field of psychology. It was also at this time that he began work on *Verbal Behavior* (1957) that was to take over twenty years to complete.

During World War II Skinner undertook two of his more famous projects. He began "Project Pigeon" when he worked with the office of Scientific Research and Development. He taught pigeons to operate the guidance system of the Pelican missile. Although they performed excellently, his Kamikaze pigeons saw no active combat. Near the end of the war Skinner and his wife had another child, Deborah. In order to make these infant years easier on parents and child, he mechanized child care with his air crib. It was basically a large glass box with temperature control and sliding glass doors. He later wrote an article on this for the *Ladies Home Journal*.

During seven weeks of the summer of 1945 Skinner wrote *Walden Two* (1948), his utopian novel about a behaviorally controlled community. At the time he seriously considered beginning such a community (Skinner, 1967).

> At one time I seriously considered an actual experiment. I could be one of the most dramatic adventurers in the twentiety century. It needs a younger man, however, and I am unwilling to give up the opportunity to do other things which in the long run may well advance the principles of *Walden Two* more rapidly. (p. 404)

In the fall of 1945 Skinner became the department chairman at Indiana University. In addition to administration he ran some experiments on pigeons and helped to found the *Journal of the Experimental Analysis of Behavior* and Division 25 of the American Psychological Association. Finally, in 1948 Skinner joined the Department of Psychology at Harvard where he conducted research and taught courses in human behavior. In the 1950's when his daughters were in school he took an interest in the educational process and this led to his development of the teaching machine. By 1958 Skinner's work had been so well received that he was honored with the American Psychological Association's Distinguished Scientific Contribution Award.

FIGURE 2

"Baby in a box" photo courtesy of B. F. Skinner

Though now in his seventies, Skinner continues to write and grant periodical interviews. Now, as in the past, he is supremely confident in his ideas and not very tolerant of his critics. At one time he said that after reading a few pages of Chomsky's *Review of Verbal Behavior,* he felt that Chomsky had missed the whole point, and refused to read any further (Hall, 1967). Likewise, it is doubtful that any of his recent critics have changed his confidence in his theory as can be seen in this quote (1967):

Behaviorism is a formulation which makes possible an effective experimental approach to human behavior. It is a working hypothesis about the nature of a subject matter. It may be clarified, but it does not need to be argued. I have no doubt of the eventual triumph of the position—not that it will eventually be proved right, but that it would provide the most direct route to a successful science of man. (pp. 409–10)

THE PLAN OF THIS BOOK This analysis of Skinner's behaviorism will begin with a look at the philosophical and scientific foundations on which the theory is built. Chapter 2 examines the philosophical assumptions from which Skinner operates as a scientist and includes a look at Skinner's view of the person, development, and psychopathology. Chapter 3 reviews the specifics of Skinner's operant conditioning theory.

Chapters 4–7 contain a critique of Skinner's behaviorism; chapter 4 examines problems with the scientific basis for Skinner's behaviorism by asking the question, Does the laboratory data support the radical behaviorism of B. F. Skinner? Chapter 5 looks at Skinner's explanation for human mental states to see if it is satisfactory in the face of rationalistic data. Chapter 6 examines the problems with Skinner's view of complete determinism. And Chapter 7 discusses the difficulty Skinner's behaviorism has with deriving value and giving direction to the proposed behavioral technology.

Many times in class, when I have been critiquing another scientist's position on an issue, my students have asked, What would so and so say to that objection, if he were here? It seems to me that it would be fair to give Skinner a chance to respond to his critics; Chapter 8, therefore, examines some of the more common objections to Skinner's behaviorism by providing answers from Skinner's own writings. Chapter 9 concludes with a look at the relationship of Christian beliefs to Skinner's behaviorism.

THE PHILOSOPHICAL FOUNDATION

No science is conducted in a **2** totally objective and unbiased fashion. Scientific data col- lection and theory generation are profoundly affected by the assumptions the scientist brings into the laboratory. In fact, even the scientist's choice of a laboratory is based on these prior assumptions! These assumptions are part of a scientist's paradigm, or world view. Since the appearance of Thomas Kuhn's *The Structure of Scientific Revolutions* (1962), scientists have been keenly aware of the effect of their philosophical assumptions on their scientific activities. In an earlier work (Cosgrove, 1979) I attempted to show that the theories of human nature and human problems in psychology are as much a product of the psychological world view under which a psychologist operates as is the research done in the laboratory. Assumptions about the nature of reality, the nature of man, and the nature of knowledge impact our views of the nature of the problems facing humanity.

The manner in which prior assumptions affect scientific activities can be divided into three categories. First, one's assumptions affect the subject matter one chooses to study. A psychologist who believes that man is only material will have a greater interest in studying human brains than haunted houses. A psychologist who believes in organic evolution should have a greater interest in comparative psychology than one who does not. Second, a scientist's assumptions affect what methods are chosen for use in the laboratory, and these methods directly affect what is discovered. For example, a psychologist who does not believe that human mental phenomena are of any consequence is more comfortable observing only the behavior of subjects. This results, however, in limiting our knowledge of humans to behaviors instead of (or in addition to) thoughts and feelings. Third, prior assumptions can affect one's interpretation of the data collected in the laboratory. A scientist who believes in an orderly cause-effect universe is more likely to interpret an ESP mind-reading experiment as subliminal perception than as extrasensory perception. Because of beliefs about reality, the scientist is predisposed to look for natural, regular causes that account for the observations.

SKINNER'S ACADEMIC ROOTS In analyzing Skinner's theoretical perspectives it is important to begin with his general assumptions as a scientist and a psychologist since these assumptions play a great role in his brand of behaviorism. It has been said that psychology has a short history but a long past, since its ideas are rooted deeply in the philosophic and scientific thinking of hundreds of years ago. Thus, it is to the historical "roots" of psychology that we must first turn, in order to understand Skinner's basic assumptions.

Empiricism and Associationism

The terms *empiricism* and *associationism* are integrally related. Empiricism refers to the sensory "writing" on the blank slate that becomes the knowledge, or the mind, which we call the person. Sensory experience, says the empiricist, is the only source of that content. However, the barrage of sensory experience to which a person is exposed is only meaningful when certain sensory inputs or stimulus inputs are associated with each other. The basic principle of association is contiguity—two experiences occurring closely together in time are likely to be associated. Stimuli may also be associated with behavioral or biological responses, and these stimulus-response (S-R) relationships become the basis for learning and personality.

FIGURE 3

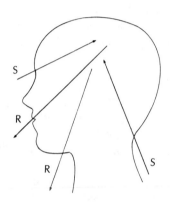

Empiricism

The "mind" is composed of S-R (stimulus-response) associations. Ideas are merely raw copies of sense data.

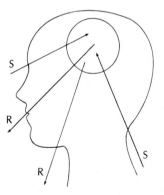

Rationalism

The mind interacts with and reflects on sense data. The question is not whether sensory experience modifies ideas but to what extent it modifies them.

A comparison of empirical and rationalistic models of knowledge and the person.

If empiricism means that all knowledge comes from the senses, then how do I know that this object in my hand is a pen? What is needed is a kind of mental glue to hold together all the stimulus sensations capable of being experienced from this object. Associationism is the glue. Stimuli and responses that occur closely together in time often enough become associated, such that one stimulus alone can cause the memory of the rest. Thus, to an empiricist, the operations of the mind, or the nature of the person, are understood by studying S-R relationships. It was with this emphasis that experimental psychology began and while Skinner does not consider himself an S-R psychologist, his empiricism lends itself to theories of learning quite similar to S-R psychology.

Pavlov and Watson

Association as a psychological principle was built into the research of both Ivan Pavlov and John B. Watson. Associationism also affected the more contemporary figures D. O. Hebb, whose cell assembly theory was an associationistic metaphor, and B. F. Skinner, whose operant conditioning theory emphasizes the association between behavior and reinforcing stimuli. Pavlov, the Nobel Prize-winning Russian physiologist, considered that the basis of associations is structural, and that repeated experiences somehow alter the structural features of activated neural elements. With his now famous classical conditioning experiments, Pavlov tried to show that not only were inborn reflexes a part of the behavior of organisms, but learned reflexes (associations) were also. These learned reflexes were formed when neutral stimuli were associated with natural stimulus-response reflexes. The neutral stimuli soon were able to elicit the reflexive responses. As a materialist and a mechanist, Pavlov was asking the question, Is it not possible that all behavior and even "mind" itself are just the combination of physiological reflexes? According to Pavlov, his experiments with dogs and salivation and the letters CS, UCS, CR, and UCR must have just now "reflexively" entered your awareness as I discussed his work.

Watson was sufficiently influenced by Pavlov's work to use the conditioned reflex as a basic building block for the theoretical construction of behavior. As the father of American psychology, Watson virtually guaranteed that psychology would take an empirical, associational direction. According to Watson, the only subject matter for psychology was behavior, since behavior could be observed. Watson cast aside terms like will, mind, awareness, desire, and idea; they were of no interest to psychology, since they could not be studied scientifically. Since Watson's behavioristic alternative is closely related to his empirical, associationistic foundations, we often use the term *behaviorist* for any psychologist who takes an empirical, mechanistic view of human nature. Actually, most psychologists consider themselves behaviorists in that they recognize the scientific advantages of using behavior as data; not all are radical behaviorists, however, since they believe in the mind, not simply as a complex stimulus-response structure, but as an innate property of a person. Thus Watson and Skinner are best considered to be "radical behaviorists." This term will be elaborated later.

Skinner's Inheritance

Although Skinner follows in the general direction of Pavlov and Watson, he does not accept classical conditioning as a paradigm of association learning. He accepts instead operant conditioning. This means that while he accepts the empirical, associationistic model of learning, he rejects the reflex learning of Pavlov, where responses are elicited by stimuli, in favor of instrumental learning, where the organism emits a response apparently at "will." Skinner's psychology, therefore, has less mechanical flavor to it than Watson's, even though he sees the organism as nonetheless determined.

Skinner also differs from the simple S-R psychology of Watson. He has incorporated E. L. Thorndike's law of effect into his theory. Thorndike felt that for most behavior there was no triggering stimulus that automatically produced behavior, but that behavior was influenced primarily by the expected consequences of that behavior. In other words, acts that have favorable consequences will recur. Skinner has added reinforcement as the critical stimulus element in any potential S-R relationships. Since it is reinforcement that *follows* behavior that becomes effective in causing that behavior to recur, Skinner's S-R theory might be written S_1-R-S_2 where S_2 is the stimulus reinforcement.

Since Watson wanted to reduce man to his physiological constructs and classical conditioning, reflex learning theory gave the impression that he denied the importance of the mind and viewed men as machines. This is not so with Skinner. He is content to reduce man to molar behavior (bar pressing, running, etc.) and admits to the operation of a mind, but insists that such a mind is formed by the same S-R-S associations that structure behavior. Therefore, Skinner's "person" turns out to be a machine that does not appear mechanized.

What Skinner does accept from his academic ancestors is as important as what he rejects. He accepts the empirical, associationistic model of man, with reinforcement as the essential stimulus ingredient in learning. With Watson, he denies the existence of the free, independent mind or soul, and accepts a description of behavior as the complete description of a person. Therefore, B. F. Skinner is very much a part of the S-R, behavioristic tradition in the United States, and is, in fact, its leading spokesman.

SKINNER'S MAJOR ASSUMPTIONS We are now prepared to examine more closely the assumptions that have shaped the nature of Skinner's theories and ideas. These assumptions involve three areas: reality, the human person, and the path to knowledge.

Naturalism and Materialism in Reality

While psychologists do not usually find it important to discuss their assumptions about the ultimate nature of reality, it is not hard to discern Skinner's beliefs. He participates in the western world's secular, scientific mentality. His current writings indicate an academic impatience toward religious beliefs; in earlier writings Skinner indicated that he was an atheist (1967). All of this suggests that he holds to a naturalistic, materialistic picture of reality. This means that he believes that the universe is composed of only matter and energy; reality does not include God, demons, souls, or other nonmaterial elements. This universe, according to naturalists, is a closed system in which every effect must have a material cause.

The importance of Skinner's naturalistic and materialistic assumptions is that they greatly limit the kinds of assumptions he can hold concerning the human mind and knowledge. If the universe is mere matter, then so is man; the human mind is only a by-product of functioning matter. If matter is ruled by laws of cause and effect, then man, who is only matter, must behave in a completely determined way. If the universe is only material, then Skinner can place great confidence in knowledge by empiricism, since there is nothing out there that is not potentially within the grasp of sensory experience.

Given Skinner's naturalistic, materialistic picture of reality, he is almost bound by consistency to believe that man is only matter, completely determined, and that scientific methods can reveal all truth about human nature. Notice that data in the laboratory have not convinced Skinner of these behavioristic views. He adheres to behaviorism first and foremost because of his materialistic and naturalistic assumptions.

Empiricism and Materialism in Man

Though Skinner believes in the material nature of the human being, (as opposed to the dualism of mind and body), he does not deny the existence of inner feelings, sensations, or thoughts. He seeks instead to clarify the nature of these functions. To Skinner these mental states are a product of environmental conditioning. He has said (1953):

> The objection to inner states is not that they do not exist, but that they are not relevant in a functional analysis. . . . The external variables of which behavior is a function provide for what may be called a causal or functional analysis. (p. 35)

Skinner believes that almost all behavior and what we call "personhood" is learned by the build-up of associations. As an empiricist, then, he is saying that personality is a product of environmental conditioning plus some relatively minor genetic predisposition. To Skinner, personality theory is just a branch of learning theory.

The following quotes from Skinner further reflect his materialistic view of the person:

> The picture which emerges from a scientific analysis is not of a body with a person inside, but of a body which *is* a person in the sense that it displays a complex repertoire of behavior. (1971, p. 190)
>
> A person is not an originating agent; he is a locus, a point at which many genetic and environmental conditions come together in a joint effect. (1974, p. 185)
>
> A behavioristic analysis rests on the following assumption: A person is first of all an organism, a member of a species and a subspecies, possessing a genetic endowment of anatomical and physiological characteristics, which are the product of contingencies of survival to which the species has been exposed in the process of evolution. The organism becomes a person as it acquires a repertoire of behavior under the contingencies of reinforcement to which it is exposed during its lifetime. The behavior it exhibits at any one moment is under the control of a current setting. (1974, p. 228)

Though Skinner believes in the existence of internal mental states and accepts some genetic influence over the behavior of an individual, he works from a strongly empirical, materialistic perspective of human nature.

Determinism in Man

Skinner believes that human behavior is basically environmentally determined. He believes that the same regularity that describes the physical world will also describe man. The laws describing human behavior are to be found in environmental factors. While Skinner admits that the research scientist is still in no position to state unequivocally that man is completely determined by his environment, he believes this is a worthwhile scientific assumption that future scientific findings will continue to validate.

Observe Skinner's own words:

> The work is mechanistic in the sense of implying a fundamental lawfullness or order in the behavior of organisms . . . but it is assumed that behavior is predictable from a knowledge of relevant variables and is free from the intervention of any capricious agent. (1938, p. 433)

When all relevant variables have been arranged, an organism will or will not respond. If it does not, it cannot. If it can, it will. To ask whether someone can turn a handspring is merely to ask whether there are circumstances under which he will do so. (1953, p. 112)

Personal exemption from a complete determinism is revoked as a scientific analysis progresses, particularly in accounting for the behavior of the individual. (1971, p. 18)

It is in the nature of an experimental analysis of human behavior that it should strip away the functions previously assigned to autonomous man and transfer them one by one to the controlling environment. (1971, p. 189)

While Skinner does not accept the mechanistic, reflex-learning model of Pavlov and Watson, he still believes in a complete determinism of human behavior.

Behaviorism and Reductionism

Skinner operates on the assumption that behaviors, not internal states, are the only acceptable data for a scientific psychology. To be truly empirical, psychology must exclude any dependent variable that cannot be directly observed. Since stimuli in the environment can be manipulated and operationally defined, whereas concepts like self, or ego, or the unconscious cannot, only behaviors and observable stimuli should constitute the subject matter of psychology. When psychologists attempt to study internal states instead of behavior, Skinner (1953) believes they are looking in the wrong place for the causes of human behavior.

The practice of looking inside the organism for an explanation of behavior has tended to obscure the variables which are immediately available for scientific analysis. These variables lie outside the organism, in its immediate environment and in its environmental history. (p. 31)

In order to scientifically study human behavior Skinner believes that the research must take place in the controlled environment of the laboratory. In addition, in order to meaningfully manipulate variables, the scientist must concentrate on simple rather than complex aspects of behavior. One can build toward explaining the complex through a study of the simple. It is also assumed by Skinner that the laws of behavior apply to both humans and animals in the same way. Therefore, he has made extensive use of rats and pigeons in the lab although he agrees that we need to confirm at least some of these findings on human subjects. Because of this methodology and his basic assumptions Skinner has been criticized as being reductionistic (MacKay, 1974). Skinner (1974) reacts against this claim, however, by denying that separate levels of description of human nature exist.

> But behaviorism does not move from one dimensional system to another. It simply provides an alternative account of the same facts. It does not *reduce* feelings to bodily states; it simply argues that bodily states are and always have been what are felt. It does not *reduce* thought processes to behavior; it simply analyzes the behavior previously explained by the invention of thought processes. It does not *reduce* morality to certain features of the social environment; it simply insists that those features have always been responsible for moral behavior. (p. 265)

This last quotation clearly identifies Skinner's brand of behaviorism. Skinner's behaviorism is not methodological behaviorism, which says that behaviorism is only a model that directs research in human and animal learning. Methodological behaviorism admits to the existence of important internal events in human beings, but says that they cannot be studied scientifically, and therefore that they are outside the domain of psychology. Skinner's radical behaviorism, on the other hand, denies the ultimate importance of the human mind by saying that it is merely the production of environmental events.

Skinner's Psychology

Skinner's assumptions make his psychological views very clear. His personality theory cannot have any structural concepts like Freud's "ego," or Rogers's "ideal self," or Eysenck's "traits." Such structures relate to relatively enduring qualities of organization, whereas the behavioral approach emphasizes the importance of stimuli in the environment.

Growth and development (in the behavioral framework) are directly related to stimuli and behavior. For example, children become more self-reliant through the reinforcement (food or praise) of behavior in which they take care of themselves. A child becomes emotionally mature through the occasional reinforcement of a stable response during which a child learns to tolerate delays in gratification.

In dealing with psychopathology Skinner considers symptoms with underlying causes as superfluous, since behavioral pathology is not a disease. There is no unconscious or "sick" personality. Pathological behavior is a response pattern learned in the same way as "normal" response patterns. If you can change the maladaptive response, you have removed the pathology. Psychological problems are merely failures in learning a proper response, or learning normal responses under the control of inappropriate reinforcers. Depression is seen as a lowered response rate. Schizophrenics might be individuals who attend to unusual cues in the environment because they are out of touch with conditions of reinforcement. Lack of emotion might be a lack of responsiveness to normal social stimuli. The job of the therapist is to deal with target behaviors, not neuroses.

In summary, this chapter has analyzed the guiding assumptions behind the work of B. F. Skinner. The examination of these assumptions provides a helpful background and foundation for understanding his scientific research.

THE SCIENTIFIC FOUNDATION

3

This chapter will briefly review Skinner's theory of operant conditioning and its accompanying technology so that we can begin our evaluation of his behaviorism with a clear understanding of his scientific methodology and the data it produces.

OPERANT CONDITIONING We will begin by distinguishing operant conditioning from classical conditioning and also from contiguity theories of learning. These differences will necessitate a slight change in the typical behavioristic S-R designation when describing Skinner's behaviorism. In classical conditioning, responses are elicited by known stimuli; the response is known as a *respondent*. The knee jerk in response to a tap on the patellar tendon and the pupillary constriction in response to light are examples. Responses that are spontaneously emitted by an organism without any correlation with known stimuli are called *operants*. Operants usually acquire a relationship with preceding stimuli. They are not *elicited* by the stimuli, but are *emitted* by the organism. Most human behavior is operant in nature. When the operant behavior emitted by the organism is made to occur regularly by the use of reinforcement, the process is called operant conditioning.[1]

There is also a difference between "merely associationistic" theories, which are known as contiguity theories, and Skinner's "more than associationistic" theory, which emphasizes reinforcement. E. R. Guthrie proposed a contiguity theory in which stimuli come to have their eliciting powers by association with responses and by association with each other. Skinner's reinforcement theory, on the other hand, incorporates the operation of reinforcement as a means of accounting for the formation of associations. The contiguity theory does not require such reinforcement.

With these differences briefly outlined between classical and operant conditioning and between contiguity and reinforcement theories, it can be seen that Skinner's operant conditioning theory is not just an ordinary S-R theory. The simple S-R designation often means that reinforcement is not a factor in the association of stimuli with responses, and the stimulus is eliciting the response. But in Skinner's theory an emitted response may occur in a particular stimulus context, but the stimuli are not the cause of the response. The reinforcement is seen as the controlling factor in the response of the organism. Therefore, instead of S-R, Skinner would prefer his theory to be simplified by S_d-R-S_{rein}, where S_d represents the discriminating stimulus, R the emitted behavior, and S_{rein} the reinforcing stimulus.

Operant Conditioning and Reinforcement

Operant conditioning simply defined means that if an operant behavior is followed by the presentation of a reinforcing stimulus, the strength of the behavior is increased. The classic example of operant conditioning is that of a rat in an operant test chamber, more commonly known as a "Skinner Box" (a name that Skinner

---

[1]The difference between operant and classical conditioning is not considered as sharp now as it once was (Hilgard and Bower, 1975, pp. 209–12), but the distinction does serve to help clarify Skinner's theory.

did not invent and detests). If a hungry rat is reinforced with food pellets when it presses a bar in its cage, bar pressing behavior will increase.

FIGURE 4

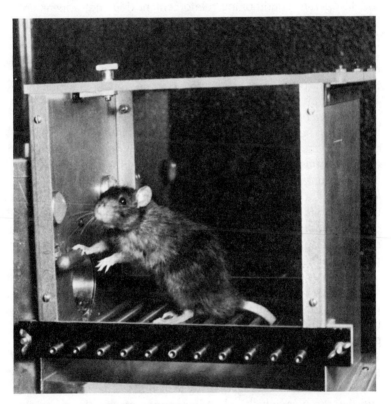

An operant test chamber (Skinner Box). Photo courtesy of B. F. Skinner.

A reinforcer therefore, is a stimulus that follows a response and increases the probability of its recurring. The reinforcer strengthens the behavior it follows. Skinner has refused to biologize the concept

of reinforcement; he has refused to "explain" what makes reinforcers reinforcing. He does not invoke homeostatic concepts like
drives, wants, hungers, and the like. What he does insist on is a
psychology that describes the functional relationships between behaviors and environmental stimuli.

In operant conditioning reinforcement does not appear until
after the appropriate response is emitted. Therefore, it is said that
reinforcement is contingent upon that response. The contingencies
of reinforcement so often spoken of by Skinner are the rules governing the relationship between responses and reinforcement.
Superstitious behavior is an example of conditioning in which there
are no systematic contingencies.

Reinforcements may be of several types: primary or secondary,
positive or negative, continuous or partial. *Primary, or unconditioned reinforcement,* is the reward to which an organism "naturally" responds. Food, water, sex, comfort, and freedom from pain
are the usual primary reinforcers. *Secondary or conditioned reinforcement* is a formerly neutral stimulus that has become reinforcing
because of its repeated association with a stimulus that is reinforcing. Secondary reinforcers will lose their reinforcing effects when
repeatedly applied to a response for which there is no eventual
primary reinforcement. Skinner would see stimuli such as money
and praise as extremely effective secondary reinforcers.

Positive reinforcement is any reinforcement that increases the
probability of the recurrence of the preceding response. Notice that
the term reinforcement is being defined in terms of its behavioral
effects. Any attempt to specify what is reinforcing on other grounds
such as need reduction is not of interest to Skinner. In particular the
physiological mechanisms involved are not a necessary part of the
science of behavior. *Negative reinforcement* is an unpleasant or
aversive stimulus, which, when removed, increases the probability
of the recurrence of the preceding response. This brings to mind the
joke about one man asking another why he was beating himself
over the head with a brick. The man's answer was, "Because it feels
so good when I quit." This illustration serves to distinguish negative
reinforcement from punishment. Negative reinforcement is rein-

forcing and serves to increase the probability of the recurrence of preceding behavior. Punishment, on the other hand, decreases the probability of a response. However, Skinner feels that the effect of punishment is temporary and appears to be of little value in eliminating behavior. For this reason he has emphasized only positive and negative reinforcement.

Continuous reinforcement is reinforcement that is associated with every response of the organism. *Partial reinforcement* is sometimes called intermittent reinforcement because not every response is followed by a reinforcer. Skinner discovered the effectiveness of this type of reinforcement quite by accident. Being low on food pellets one day, he set up his animal apparatus for partial reinforcement, and even more responding was observed. One final term related to the concept of reinforcement is *extinction*. When a behavior is no longer followed by a reinforcement, that behavior will weaken and eventually stop. The rate of this extinction is a function of the past history of reinforcement for that behavior.

THE CONDITIONING OF COMPLEX BEHAVIOR It is easy to see how operant conditioning works in simple behavior like bar pressing. The animal makes a response, is reinforced and subsequently learns to make that response with increasing frequency. Understanding how operant conditioning works with complex behaviors is more difficult since there are many behaviors that one would never expect to be emitted spontaneously and therefore could never be reinforced. You might, for example, expect your dog to chase cars, but it is doubtful that he would ever spontaneously get your slippers and lay them beside your easy chair. How, therefore, can reinforcement be applied to this complex behavior? The answer is found in the concepts of *shaping* and *chaining*.

Shaping is the conditioning of a complex behavior by reinforcing gradual approximations of that desired response. In our example of the dog and your slippers, for example, you might begin to produce slipper-getting behavior by at first reinforcing any movement of the dog in the direction of the slippers. Then, withhold reinforcement until the dog emits a few steps toward the slippers. Then, again withhold reinforcement until it is sniffing and pushing at the slippers. In this way you are gradually shaping the dog's behavior toward the desired response.

Another way complex behavior can be produced by operant conditioning is by the method of response chaining. In chaining, a sequence of individual behavioral responses is assembled into a performance unit. The successive stimuli in the chain act as descriminative stimuli for responding in their presence and as secondary reinforcers for the responses that precede them. An example of a chained response is the complex sequence of behaviors that circus animals perform. Each of the individual behaviors that constitute the eventual "act" are reinforced and then are linked with others to compose the total response.

APPLICATIONS OF SKINNER'S BEHAVIORISM The applications of the principles of operant conditioning have been numerous and varied. Operant conditioning has been used to speed up animal learning, improve patient behavior in psychiatric wards, improve school learning, cure problems like stuttering and bed wetting, remove disruptive or delinquent behavior, teach the self-control of unwanted habits, and do other useful things.

One of Skinner's most novel applications was the teaching machine and programmed learning in the field of education. While teaching machines have not replaced teachers, they and programmed learning texts are widely used today. Although Skinner did not invent the teaching machine, which was patented over one-hundred years ago, he did give us its modern form. The teaching machine emphasizes immediate reinforcement when a correct response is emitted by a student; it helps shape complex responses. The modern teaching machine consists of a window to display questions or statements in which a word has been left out. After a question is asked, the student must write in an answer, and then pull a lever to reveal the correct answer. Reinforcement is obtained because the machine then moves ahead to the next question. If the student is correct, he or she moves to the next item.

In therapy, behavior modification techniques based upon operant conditioning have been used extensively to cure obesity, asthma, stuttering, phobias, anti-social acts, marital difficulties, depression, alcoholism, drug addiction, fetishism, auditory hallucinations, schizophrenic behavior, childhood autism, mental retardation, and other pathological behaviors. The list seems almost endless. In general, behavior modification proceeds by arranging contingencies in the environment so that undesirable behavior is not reinforced but desirable behavior is. This may sound simple, but the identification and manipulation of relevant reinforcing agents in the existing environment can be exceedingly difficult.

Language skills have also been effectively taught to autistic children using behavior modification techniques. Prompts, food, and praise reinforcements have been used very effectively to shape these children's attending behavior and simple vocalizations into into meaningful language.

Behavior modification principles have been applied to large groups of individuals by the use of token economies, techniques in which tokens, such as plastic chips or credit cards that can be punched, act as secondary reinforcers that can be converted into primary reinforcers. The system, which can generally only be applied in highly controlled environmental settings like hospitals, prisons, or classrooms, usually operates on a contract basis and the person is informed of what behavior is expected for the tokens. Some economies even require tokens for meals! Other large scale applications of behavior modification techniques are occurring today in the form of reinforcements given for car pooling or the control of littering.

At this time the application of operant conditioning principles to the whole of society is speculative and utopian, and because of the difficulties involved in such applications, they might forever remain mere speculations. Skinner, however, is hopeful and has outlined the potential for the behavioral management of an entire society in *Beyond Freedom and Dignity* (1971), and *Walden Two* (1948). *Walden Two* makes very interesting reading for students of human behavior but it is not terribly exciting as a novel, since like most utopian books, it has no plot; it is basically a guided tour and lecture. In the book Skinner's alter-ego and designer of *Walden Two*, Frazier, discusses the details of the behaviorally managed community and the dreams of applying such principles to entire nations and even the world.

Some of Skinner's optimism concerning the use of the principles of behaviorism for the management of society can be seen in the fact that *Walden Two* was written shortly after the "pigeons in a pelican" project was terminated. Skinner (1961) comments on this:

> In the year which followed the termination of Project Pigeon I wrote *Walden Two*, a utopian picture of a properly engineered society. Some psychotherapists might argue that I was suffering from personal rejection and simply retreated to a fantasied world where everything went according to plan, and where there never was heard a discouraging word. But another explanation is, I think, equally plausible. That piece of science fiction was a declaration of confidence in a technology of behavior. Call it a crackpot idea if you will; it is one in which I have never lost faith. I still believe that the same kind of wide-ranging speculation about human affairs, supported by studies of compensatory rigor, will make a substantial contribution toward that world of the future in which, among other things, there will be no need for guided missiles. (p. 426.18)

Having briefly presented the major features of Skinner's behaviorism and its application, we will now begin both a more thorough presentation and critical analysis of these ideas. Chapter 4 will begin our evaluation by looking at some of the general scientific problems Skinner's behaviorism presents.

THE SCIENTIFIC LIMITS

One of the greatest difficulties **4** in evaluating Skinner's theoretical perspectives is that of deciding what the grounds of the evaluation will be. Most of Skinner's critics do not quarrel with his scientific methods or his data, but rather with the philosophical weaknesses and the broader attempts at applying his behavioristic theory to complex human functioning. Specifically, Skinner's critics have suggested that behavioristic methods can never give an adequate view of human nature and that it is impossible to generalize and apply to human principles of behavior observed in simple animals. Skinner responds to such philosophical criticisms by saying that his science is being misunderstood. Therefore Skinner sets up a dichotomy between science and philosophy.

Unfortunately, when this happens it seems that we are forced to choose between the clear, objective data of the scientific laboratory, and obtuse, ancient, armchair speculation. Given this as a choice, of course, many people feel impelled to go along with what science has purportedly proven about human nature rather than accept religious or philosophical viewpoints. The position taken by this author is that the dichotomy is artificial, and that it is not only feasible but actually essential that our scientific work be carried out within the framework of one or more broad philosophical or religious views of reality and human nature.

The best scientist is the one who knows what the scientific tools can or cannot do. Therefore, it is *scientific* criticism to look carefully at the limits of Skinner's scientific methods as well as at its contributions. It is essential to ask philosophical questions because all science is carried out in the midst of philosophical assumptions and speculations. The data one selects for study, the subjects one uses, the problems studied, and the methods used to study problems all reflect basic assumptions and religious and philosophical perspectives. If one is a poor philosopher, or if the philosophical underpinning of one's scientific endeavors are not made explicit, then that person's science is bound by the same poverty.

This chapter will focus on three perceived limits to Skinner's behaviorism as a science: (1) the limits of empirical, behavioristic methods in studying human nature, (2) the limits of generalizations from simple behaviors and animal subjects, and (3) the limits of a behaviorism that has historically isolated itself from most other forms of psychology.

THE LIMITS OF BEHAVIORISTIC KNOWLEDGE

In analyzing a scientific system of thought it is of value to ask questions regarding the particulars of the method of knowing in that system. The method of knowing chosen by the behaviorist is empiricism, knowledge solely from sensory experience. This choice obviously has much to commend it since behavior can be observed, whereas thought or emotions cannot be so directly studied. The question asked here, however, is, What kind of restrictions has behaviorism placed on itself by limiting the study of human nature to the study of human behavior?

The Positivist Approach

Skinner (1938) has defined the epistemological roots of his own system as positivistic.

> So far as scientific method is concerned, the system set up in the
> preceding chapter is as follows. It is positivistic. It confines itself
> to description rather than explanation. (p. 44)

Positivism is a philosophical position intended to set limits to philosophical inquiry and thus avoid meaningless discussion. Positivism says that only statements that have meaning, that is, those that can be empirically verified through sense experience, are worth discussing. The statement, "There is oxygen in this jar," is meaningful because it can be verified empirically. However, the statement, "Adultery is immoral," is meaningless because it cannot be empirically verified. In fact, according to positivism, statements about God, mind, evil, freedom, wrong, and other similar subjects are in this meaningless category, and consequently, it would be a waste of time and effort to discuss them.

One major problem with positivism is that it destroys itself by its own definition of what constitutes a meaningless statement. The basic proposition of positivism is, Only factual statements that can be verified by sense experience are meaningful; any other kind of statement is meaningless jibberish. According to this proposition, positivism is meaningless jibberish since its basic proposition cannot be verified by a sense experience! This is similar to a teacher trying to communicate that all communication is impossible; in the very act of communicating the theory, the teacher would negate it. Positivism also negates itself in that, if it is true that empirically unverifiable statements are meaningless, then the statements of positivism itself must also be meaningless, since they cannot be empirically verified.

A second criticism of positivism that relates to a problem with Skinner's positivistic behaviorism is that positivism represents a self-imposed intellectual ignorance. So much of reality is beyond discussion or study, that we are in danger of limiting our study to the trivial. The great themes of life, religion, value, purpose, and evil are relegated from discussion. In behaviorism the *activities* of persons may be studied, but the *essence* of humanity is lost from view by this positivistic influence.

Empiricism and behaviorism are obviously related to positivistic thinking in that they, too, are self-imposed intellectual restrictions. The empiricist says we can only learn truth by sense experience. Some more radical formulations of empiricism state that the only reality that exists is that which is empirically verifiable. Interestingly, there is no way to empirically verify this statement! It has to be accepted on faith. We should be very skeptical of any system that contradicts itself in its own explanation of reality.

Beginning the study of psychology with such a hard-headed empirical approach is often considered essential and very scientific. Actually, the statements made by radical empiricism might be considered unscientific when the inherent dogma is considered and contrasted with the humility that should characterize the scientific search. Philosopher Elton Trueblood reflected on this idea (Trueblood, 1973):

> . . . science at its best is very humble in the face of nature and the ultimate mysteries. Science asks questions and accepts evidence of all kinds without judging the situation in advance. To say that we cannot know objective reality except by means of sense experience is clearly to prejudge the case. It is, therefore, *unscientific*. (p. 197)

The Behavioristic Approach

Skinner's behaviorism also suffers the danger of being considered unscientific because, in the effort to make sure that he knows something about human nature that is without error, Skinner may have left himself with very little knowledge of human nature at all. Limiting the study of human nature to the study of human behavior precludes ever getting a complete picture. In fact, it has left the psychology books with discussions that relate very little to human nature. Topics such as human motivation, thinking, creativity, subconscious, emotion, aspiration, prejudice, and others are essentially lost to the behaviorist; to say that they do not exist is to prejudge the case. Redefining these elements of human nature in terms of human behavior may aid in understanding them, but descriptions of the relationship of certain behaviors to environmental contingencies falls short of explaining their nature and origin. Skinner's discussions about the contents and operations of the mind, the nature of freedom, and personality are limited by the behaviors and reinforcing stimuli he can observe. It is no wonder that he fails to find "person" and "freedom"; his method cannot measure such things. When he says that these do not exist, he is failing to recognize the limits of his method of knowing.

Operationalism

Psychology's method for achieving empirical descriptions of psychological subject matter is through the use of operational definitions. An operantional definition is a definition in terms of some easily identifiable behavioral operation; it is usually quantifiable. Psychological research could not be conducted without the use of operational definitions, but the same research is limited to the validity of its operational terms. For example, instead of dealing with the nebulous concept of love in an experiment, a researcher might define ten dates with the same person or sexual intimacy as love. An angry person could be operationally identified by that person's harsh words. One of the difficulties with operational terms is the frequent need to operationally define the operational definitions. What exactly is meant by a date? Does an unplanned meeting in the park qualify? What is meant by harsh words? Is a swear word indicative of anger or disappointment? And might not the same word have different meanings and communicate different emotional states for different people at different times? The fact that there are numerous definitions of *anxiety* is a case in point. One researcher may operationally define anxiety through the use of MMPI scales, while another may define it in terms of the measurement of the Galvanic Skin Response. And these two different measures of anxiety may correlate little with each other!

A more pertinent question about operational terms concerns the behavioral definition's ability to specify the nature of a psychological phenomenon. When psychological phenomena are defined in terms of observable behaviors, something of the essence of what is being defined is lost. When a behaviorist summarizes his research in a textbook by saying that love is a product of the environment, he is really saying that *his operational definition of love* is a product of the environment. The value of psychological research depends upon how close a relationship actually exists between the mental event and the behavioral definition of the mental event.

Since human mental states are so difficult to define operationally, many behaviorists simply refuse to study psychological variables, saying that they cannot be empirically investigated. A behaviorist, therefore, ought to be agnostic about his ability to study the existence, meaning, and importance of internal mind states. If the internal state that is of interest is undefinable, then it cannot be studied or related to the environment.

Skinner, however, is not at all agnostic about human mental states! He assumes that his behavioral definitions of mental states are equal to the supposed psychological states. In this way he can claim to be an authority on such states and still remain an empiricist. But, with this approach Skinner is assuming the very thing that he says his science is proving, that is, he assumes that mental states are unimportant correlates of behaviors, and then after much research on mental states (subject behaviors), he declares that mental states are merely behaviors.

This discussion of operational definitions and behaviorism was not meant to criticize their use in psychology, for they are essential. But we must recognize their limits and realize that our experimentation and theorizing is only as accurate as our operational definitions; the definitions must define reality. Skinner's definitions of mental phenomena are potentially far removed from human emotions and thinking, and therefore, his research results lose some of their explanatory power.

Noam Chomsky, an open critic of Skinner's behaviorism, has pointed out an example of behaviorism's problem with operational definitions. The concept of reinforcement is defined by the behaviorist as any stimulus that can act to increase the probability of a recurrence of a response of an organism. This is a circular definition that serves to protect the operant conditioning model from ever being shown to be incorrect. If a behaviorist is asked why an animal or human failed to respond in the presence of a reinforcing stimulus (i.e., Might your theory be wrong?), the answer given is that it is obvious that the stimulus was not a reinforcer for this orgnaism because the organism failed to respond. But, this is again a case of assuming in one's operational definition what one wants to show, and it completely removes the possibility that the theory can be proven wrong. If a food reward fails to increase a rat's behavior, rather than doubting the truth of operant conditioning theory the behaviorist merely has to say that it is obvious (since operant conditioning theory is true) that the food couldn't have been a reinforcer in this case, or otherwise the rat would have performed. But what we are trying to determine is whether or not reinforcement does control behavior, therefore, the behaviorist shouldn't assume that reinforcement does control behavior in his very definition of reinforcement. This is clearly a case of assuming in one's argument the very point to be proven. In other words, the behaviorist assumes in his operational definition of reinforcement the truth of operant conditioning theory. This is not good science. If a theory is not falsifiable, it is no longer an acceptable scientific theory. Chomsky (1959) summarizes this point with respect to verbal behavior.

> It seems that Skinner's claim that all verbal behavior is acquired and maintained in "strength" through reinforcement is quite empty, because his notion of reinforcement has no clear content, functioning only as a cover term for any factor, detectable or not, related to the acquisition or maintenance of behavior. (p. 226)

THE LIMITS OF GENERALIZING FROM THE SIMPLE AND THE ANIMAL

There is most certainly a place in psychology for the investigation of simple behaviors before proceding to complex ones. A valid case can also be made for using animals as subjects and generalizing some of the findings to humans. Studying simple behaviors and using animal subjects in experimentation allow for a greater degree of control than is possible with complex variables or human subjects. There is a serious question, however, about the heavy reliance Skinner has placed upon the investigation of simple animal behaviors as a basis for his philosophical pronouncements about the nature of human freedom, motivation, learning, psychopathology, and so forth. Skinner's willingness to generalize far beyond the data was seen in his first book. Despite the fact that it was almost exclusively about rats in bar pressing situations, it was called *The Behavior of Organisms*. While there has been some operant conditioning research done on higher animals and humans, it is quite clear that it has not been Skinner's priority to extend his research efforts into complex variables and on human subjects before announcing discoveries about human nature.

Skinner, however, assumes that any complex behavior, even a human behavior, is composed of an assemblage of simpler behaviors that can be shown to be learned by operant conditioning. He also assumes that the principles of learning found in the animal, particularly the rat and the pigeon, are identical to the principles of learning behind all human behavior. He says in his own defense (Skinner, 1974), "Enough has been done to suggest that the same basic processes occur in both animals and men" (p. 250).

The problem with these two assumptions is that Skinner is again assuming the very points that are in question. Skinner *assumes* that complex human behaviors are just an assemblage of simple behaviors. For this reason he confines his studies to simple animal behaviors, and then feels perfectly safe to generalize his animal results to explain complex human behaviors. What is needed is research to shed light on this question and not pronouncements to the effect that science has demonstrated the behaviorist's model of human nature! First, there should be extensive research on the operant conditioning of primates to determine if the basic principles formulated on rats and pigeons remain valid. Second, though it is difficult, more behavioristic research needs to be done on humans to isolate the supposed controlling primary and secondary reinforcers responsible for complex human functions, such as creative, verbal, and moral behaviors.

It is essential to realize that Skinner has not made a *scientific* discovery to the effect that all human behavior is the product of environmental conditioning. He has hardly studied humans or the behaviors most in question. He has run very selective experiments showing conditioning, has made no attempt to design an experiment to disprove his basic thesis on human nature, and it is doubtful that any human data produced could not be reduced to his ambiguous behavioristic language explaining it away. Consequently there are serious doubts about his "scientific" discovery that all the accomplishments of human life from simple, physical reflexes to the construction of a poem could be successfully reduced to bits of operantly conditioned behavior. Skinner is safest in his assumptions about human behavior when he talks about behaviors also seen in the rat, and least safe in the areas of private human mental life that we cannot directly investigate.

Skinner's generalizations from research are also limited by the experimental situations and equipment he has chosen to concentrate on. The tightly controlled environment of the Skinner Box greatly limits the range of behaviors a rat can demonstrate. There are very few responses that the Skinner Box is equipped to record. The responses one chooses to observe in an animal dictate a great deal of the kind of theory one can hold in psychology. Tolman and Kohler's research on animal learning broadened the environmental context in which animals could operate; they learned that certain animal behavior was not at all related to the contingencies of reinforcement in the history of the animal but rather to variables like insight and cognitive maps.

Learning psychologist James McConnell (1977) has written a short science fiction story about a learning theorist who was captured and transferred to a spaceship. His captors were alien psychologists who planned to observe him as an "animal" specimen. They placed him in a research box to see if all of their favorite learning theories would describe his behavior. As this human learning theorist was traveling through space going who knows where, his captors were conducting operant conditioning experiments on him. He was terribly frustrated by this situation because the restrictiveness of the experimental apparatus and the food deprivation virtually guaranteed that he would perform according to conditioning theory. He had no way to demonstrate his advanced cognitive abilities. He also realized that if he did make his abilities known, he would no longer be performing according to theory and might be sacrificed as a "sick" specimen.

McConnell's story is only fiction, but, according to E. C. Tolman, rats in different circumstances can show cognitive approaches to learning. In a very real sense the whole of human nature is limited by what Skinner's subjects can do in his box of empirical restrictions.

THE LIMITS OF AN ISOLATED BEHAVIORISM

Another major problem for behaviorism is Skinner's unwillingness to work through some of the solid data and theories of other psychologies that run counter to his own. The reason is not that Skinner is unaware of the other theories and data, but that behaviorism is limited, in the interests of being "scientific," to a particular view of human nature and knowledge; no serious consideration is given to other scientific areas of psychology.

Psychology in the form of behaviorism won the hard-fought battle to become an empirical science by initially rejecting the introspection of Wundt and the rationalistic concepts of Wertheimer's Gestalt psychology. So, too, today when any competing psychological system utilizes methods that are less empirical than behaviorism, or invokes explanations with a rationalistic or mentalistic leaning, they are simply ignored. The scientific "objectivity" of behaviorism has been won at the expensive price of isolation from most nonbehavioristic systems including physiological psychology. Daniel Robinson (1979) in his excellent treatment of systems of modern psychology, described this problem of Skinner's behaviorism this way:

> The problem is that as a purely descriptive enterprise with official sanctions against biological and cognitive theorizing, it is not equipped even in principle to embrace such subjects and processes. (p. 140)

The problem for Skinner is that a massive amount of scientific research in other areas of psychology supports a more rationalistic picture of man. Well-established areas like Piaget's stage theory, Gestalt psychology, Tolman's purposive behaviorism and modern cognitive psychology, Karl Lashley's principle of mass action in physiological psychology, studies in ethology, and Chomsky's language development theory all speak out against the associationistic, empirical model of man in Skinner's radical behaviorism. Skinner's behaviorism faces the pressure to change, since it is difficult to reduce all of these kinds of data to a behavioristic system. Skinner does not come to terms with these psychologies simply because his system must reject the kinds of theoretical constructs they use. In the next chapter I will consider the data and theories of some of these psychologies that run counter to Skinner's behaviorism.

Skinner's behaviorism also fails to explain some additional findings of operant conditioning experiments. For example, two former associates of Skinner, Keller and Marion Breland, used their training in operant conditioning to establish an animal training business. In 1960 they published a whimsical paper in the *American Psychologist* entitled, "The Misbehavior of Organisms," which detailed the contingencies of reinforcement that did not succeed entirely in controlling what the animals did. Animals often did things they were not reinforced for. These "misbehaviors" seemed to be species-specific, food-related behaviors. It appears that members of a species are instinctively "prepared" to make certain learned attachments. In another article entitled "Learning Theory—Two Trials and Tribulations," Freedman, Cohen, and Hennessy (1974) reversed the hypothesis of Skinner and showed that a behavior followed by a reinforcement is likely not to be repeated. This kind of data needs to be seriously considered in evaluating the adequacy of Skinner's model of learning.

Another problem with Skinner's model of operant conditioning is his emphasis on proximate external consequences as controllers of behavior. Countless human studies have demonstrated that consequences do not have to be immediate for humans to learn. Because a human being represents things symbolically he is able to bring his behavior under the control of distant consequences through anticipatory thought. The principles of observational learning have been well established (Bandura, 1971) and illustrate that humans and animals can learn with delayed reinforcement because they are able to "hold" learning as a central event rather than as a peripheral event tied up in some musculature response. None of these kinds of findings are anticipated by the principles of operant conditioning.

SUMMARY   In conclusion, it seems that while certain aspects of Skinner's behaviorism pose significant problems, his system is so exclusive that it attempts to exclude all possible criticism. Skinner's scientific work has clearly amassed a great deal of data and contributed immensely to our understanding of behavior, especially animal behavior. He clearly deserves the recognition he has received as one of the foremost psychological scientists of this century.

When Skinner theorizes about the meaning of his data, however, he repeatedly makes grand inferences about human behavior from studies of animals. His methods, by their very nature, exclude observations about unique, human experiences (if such, in fact, exist!). His "science" has also been conducted within a circular, theoretical logic that rules out the possibility of change in the light of other theories and data. Consequently Skinner's science has a tendency to become scientism; he has traded the humility of knowledge for the rigidity of dogma.

THE QUESTION OF MIND

In addition to the problems **5** that arise because of Skinner's generalization and applica- tion of animal responses to human behavior and the limi- tations of his methodology for studying complex human functions, another problem has plagued S-R psychologies since the days of Watson. That problem is the mounting evidence for the existence of important, inner, controlling, mental or cognitive states in human beings. These states alter stimuli and help generate responses. In other words, quite apart from religious and philosophical views on the nature of man, there is psychological evidence that indicates that the control of the person comes not only from the outside environment but also from the inner person.

Problems for Watson's S-R psychology developed early when Wertheimer published his findings on the phi phenomenon, and when Gestalt psychology began its study of perceptual illusions. The phi phenomenon is a simple illusion, in which two lights blinking alternately appear as one light moving from side to side. The problem with this observation for any S-R psychology is that the experience or response is obviously not just a function of the stimulus input. In the physical world there are two blinking lights; in the world of experience there is only one moving light. It is clear that something must be intervening between stimulus and response that actively changes the stimulus into the response observed. After such demonstrations Gestalt psychologists felt that the important variables in human behavior were internal and not external. Other Gestalt examples are forms such as a square; Why are its four lines seen as a square—something greater than the sum of the parts? Or, consider the Müller-Lyer illusion. This well-known illusion involves two horizontal lines of identical length; one has arrowheads that point inward and the other has arrowheads that point outward. The illusion is that the line with the inward pointing arrowheads is decidedly longer. Again, the stimulus cannot be related to the response without positing an important, active, internal state that manipulates stimulus input.

FIGURE 5

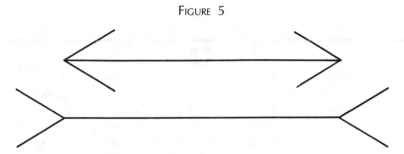

The Müller-Lyer illusion. The line with the outgoing arrowheads appears to be longer than the line with the ingoing arrowheads.

The problems for S-R psychologists do not end with a few illusions from Gestalt psychologists. The research of sensory psychology in areas as diverse as human pattern perception and social perception has yielded the unshakeable thesis that one's perceptual experience is only in a small way the product of the stimulus world. The most important variables in perception have been shown to be memory, expectation, motivation, and attention. American behaviorism has been further beleaguered by onslaughts from a diverse number of research areas such as Wolfgang Kohler's insight learning in apes, Jean Piaget's rationalistic stage theory, and Noam Chomsky's nativistic evidences in language acquisition. Karl Lashley's principle of mass action was a watershed principle, shifting physiological psychology away from associationistic, synaptic theories of learning and memory. American behavioristic learning theory itself was in a rapid movement toward the intervening variables (i.e., variables between S and R) of Clark Hull's learning theory, and the "purposive" behaviorism of E. C. Tolman, whose discussion of cognitive maps and latent learning made psychologists reconsider the "mind" of the rat.

This, then, was the psychological climate in which Skinner developed a behaviorism rooted in the Watsonian empirical view of human nature. Consequently, it has been of utmost importance for Skinner to de-emphasize his theory's relationship with traditional stimulus-response psychology. Since he emphasizes the concept of reinforcement, Skinner considers his behaviorism to be not an S-R psychology but an S-R-S psychology. More specifically it is an S^d-R-S^{rein} psychology, in which S^d is the discriminative stimulus and S^{rein} is the reinforcing stimulus. Skinner holds that his theory is not an S-R theory in the sense of a Watsonian theory of stimuli eliciting responses. To Skinner the organism emits a response (in the context of a stimulus environment), which is controlled by the following reinforcing stimulus. This difference between Skinner and Watson is clear, but the question remains how an S^d-R-S^{rein} psychology avoids the problem of explaining internal mental states as an important part of the person. The only avenue open to Skinner is to include these internal states as part of the R, that is, these internal thoughts, motivations, and feelings, that seem so obviously to have a role in human behavior, are as much a product of the conditioning environment as the visible behaviors of the person.

We can summarize Skinner's position on this issue as follows: Skinner's behaviorism says that all behavior is a product of the environment. Other research, however, shows that internal variables of mind play a major role in human behavior. Skinner then counters that these mental variables, too, are shaped and controlled by the environment according to principles of operant conditioning.

Because of the demonstrated limitation of S-R psychology, Skinner has extended his theory to describe the conditioning of internal mind states. While not denying the existence of internal states, he has sought to reinterpret them and to set his views apart from traditional S-R psychology. For this reason a great deal of the content of Skinner's recent books has been devoted to the defense of his position on mental phenomenon. In fact, his *Science and Human Behavior* (1953), *Verbal Behavior* (1957), *Beyond Freedom and Dignity* (1971), and *About Behaviorism* (1974) read like an effort to save behaviorism from cognitive psychology. In the Preface (June, 1966) to the seventh printing of *The Behavior of Organisms* (1938), Skinner reviewed his approach to S-R psychology and cognitive variables quite clearly.

> *The Behavior of Organisms* is often placed quite erroneously in the S-R tradition. The book remains committed to the program stated in my 1931 paper in which the stimulus occupied no special place among the independent variables. The simplest contingencies involve at least three terms—stimulus, response, and reinforcer—and at least one other variable (the deprivation associated with the reinforcer) is implied. This is very much more than input and output, and when all relevant variables are thus taken into account, there is no need to appeal to an inner apparatus, whether mental, psychological, or conceptual. The contingencies are quite enough to account for attending, remembering, learning, forgetting, generalizing, abstracting, and many so called cognitive processes. In the same way, histories of satiation and deprivation take the place of internalized drives, schedules of reinforcement account for sustained probabilities of responding otherwise attributed to dispositions of traits and so on. (p. xii)

While the evidence cited against Skinner's behaviorism has not forced him to radically change his theory, it has, nonetheless forced him to clarify it and to acknowledge that mental events have to be explained. But the question remains, Can Skinner demonstrate that all mental events are indeed a product of the environment?

SKINNER'S VIEW OF THE MIND   Skinner's radical behaviorism suggests that we can have direct access to internal mental events because they are controlled by the same environmental contingencies that cause outward behaviors. For Skinner, observable behavior (including physiological responses) is the stuff of which internal states are constructed. First a person responds, and then the physical bodily response and its interpretation become the internal "mind state" of the person. By studying the external behaviors responsible for internal states one can learn about the internal states themselves. This viewpoint is very closely related to the James-Lange theory of emotions, which says that one's bodily feelings during autonomic nervous system arousal are the emotions one experiences and learns to call mental states.

Skinner does not deny the existence of inner emotions, thoughts, or motivations, but he does seek to redefine them. Skinner says that a thought is simply a sensing of one's own behavior. Unfortunately, according to Skinner, we have for centuries mislabeled these feelings as the "mind's content," and since we insist on attributing behavior to this inner person, we resist any technology of behavior control. He writes (Skinner, 1974):

> Feelings are not the causes of behavior. But what are the feelings made of? We usually say mind. To get a child to eat we deprive him of food (physical event) and then he feels hungry (mental event) and then he eats (physical event). The question is how did the food deprivation cause the feelings and how did those feelings cause behavior. (p. 11)

Thought, says Skinner (1957)

> is simply *behavior,* verbal or nonverbal, covert or overt. It is not some mysterious process responsible for behavior but the very behavior itself in all the complexity of its controlling relations. (p. 449)

In *About Behaviorism* (1974) he writes,

> Mental life and the world in which it is lived are inventions. They have been invented on the analogy of external behavior occurring under external contingencies. Thinking is behaving. (p. 115)

His view of the self inside the skin is:

> A self is a repertoire of behavior appropriate to a given set of contingencies. (1971, p. 189)
>   Self is simply a device for representing a *functionally unified set of responses*. (1953, p. 285)

All these quotations show that, while Skinner believes in the existence of the mind, he relegates it to the category of feelings during behavior. *Mental states do not initiate behavior but are caused by it. And, in the same way that the environment controls a person's behavior, it also controls his thinking and feelings.* This view of the mind suffers from the same problems as some of Skinner's other conclusions; there is no evidence to support it. Although it is an option, the case for Skinner's view of mental phenomena is not based on human laboratory research but on his theoretical assumptions, and on the generalization of his operant conditioning principles to make them apply to complex human activity.

Consider a man who plays eighteen holes of golf every week *hoping* to break a score of eighty. Shall we say he is "hoping" to do this or do the "contingencies of partial reinforcement" explain his behavior? Feelings of hope and cognition, Skinner says, should be explained as collaterals of behavior and not initiators of it. But the question needs to be answered, can Skinner actually show that thought is conditioned? Are the contingencies of reinforcement supposed by Skinner supported by persuasive evidence? Has any attempt been made to identify the primary and secondary reinforcement histories behind such a man's mental state? Anyone who has read *Science and Human Behavior* (1953), *Beyond Freedom and Dignity* (1971), and *About Behaviorism* (1974) can clearly see that Skinner does not rely on carefully developed data (from, for example, extinction and secondary reinforcement or shaping and chaining) for his explanation of mental states. Yet, if his view of mind is correct, we should be able to find such precise data in our investigation of human mental behavior. Noam Chomsky in his "Review of Skinner's *Verbal Behavior*" (1959) said,

What has been hoped for from the psychologist is some indication how the casual and informal description of everyday behavior in the popular vocabulary can be explained or clarified in terms of the notions developed in careful experiment and observation, or perhaps replaced in terms of a better scheme. A mere terminological revision, in which a term is used with the full vagueness of the ordinary vocabulary is of no conceivable interest. . . . It seems that Skinner's claim that all verbal behavior is acquired and maintained in "strength" through reinforcement is quite empty, because his notion of reinforcement has no clear content, functioning only as a cover term for any factor, detectable or not, related to the acquisition or maintenance of behavior. (pp. 226–27)

JAMES-LANGE REVISITED Skinner's theory of human mental states is very similar to the James-Lange theory of emotions. This theory said that, when a person felt an emotion, what they were feeling was the arousal of their body's autonomic nervous system. A classic example of this would be the feeling of fear one has on meeting a bear in the woods. According to the James-Lange theory, what is labeled as fear is the person's automatic "fight or flight" response of the sympathetic nervous system, which increases the heart and breathing rates. This theory was largely discredited because it can be shown that quadriplegic humans or rats (paralyzed from the neck down and having no feelings from their autonomic nervous system) still exhibit and report emotional feelings. It also seems that the body's physiological arousal is much too generalized and brief to explain human emotions.

While our emotions are certainly related to our autonomic arousal, it is by no means clear that our thinking and willing and other internal mental states are also. When trying to extend his theory to human thinking, Skinner gives examples of sensory discrimination, sensory abstraction, and sensory memories as internal states that can be related to sensory feeling. But, these do not exhaust the inner world of the creative, imaginative, reasoning, thinking mind. No one wishes to claim that thinking is not *influenced* by our environment, but is it not rash to suggest that it is equal to the environment's effect on our bodies?

RATIONALISTIC PSYCHOLOGY   To continue our look at the limitations of Skinner's view of the mind, we will now review several major psychological findings that appear to conflict with it.

The scientists cited would all consider themselves behaviorists in the sense that they often use behavior as their prime or exclusive dependent variable in scientific research. But they have not accepted the empirical, blank slate view of man of Skinner's radical behaviorism, which converts all talk about mind into descriptions of behavior. The following scientific findings can, therefore, be considered in support of the rationalist tradition in psychology.

Latent Learning and Cognitive Maps—E. C. Tolman

One of the earliest attacks on radical behavioristic theories was that of E. C. Tolman. After his studies on latent learning Tolman decided that people and animals could do things in the apparent absence of discriminative stimuli (Tolman, 1948, 1967). In latent learning experiments animals are exposed to an environment, but are not reinforced for any behavior emitted in that environment. In later testing with reinforcement these animals proved to be superior to animals that had not previously been exposed to the environment. This experiment showed that learning was taking place all along in the "mind" of the animal. Even when the rats were placed on little carts and wheeled through the maze, learning occurred. It became apparent, then, that reinforcement is necessary for performance but not for learning.

To explain his rats' abilities to improve by mere exposure to the test situation, Tolman developed the concept of "cognitive maps." He felt that the animals were forming a map of the environment in their heads rather than learning motor responses in the presence of certain stimuli. The simple explanation of associating a stimulus and a response will not explain how a rat that is wheeled through a maze can correctly run through the maze, or how a rat that is trained to run through the maze can also swim correctly through it. It is apparent that these animals are learning things in the absence of discriminative stimuli and their attachments to certain responses.

FIGURE 6

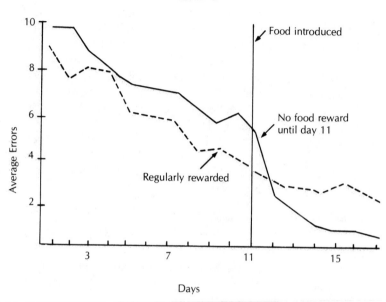

The results of a latent-learning experiment where animals were rewarded after a period of non-reward. Their performance showed that they had been learning even without reinforcement (after Tolman and Honzik, 1930).

Tolman also observed vicarious trial-and-error behavior in animals at choice points in their learning tasks. The animal was observed to hesitate and visibly compare the alternative stimuli before making a choice. The active comparison of discriminative stimuli again seems to indicate cognitive processes at work at these choice points.

Insight Learning—Wolfgang Kohler

Kohler ran a series of experiments during the years 1913–17 on the island of Tenerife, off the coast of Africa, which challenged American behavioristic psychology (Kohler, 1925). In one experiment an ape had two sticks, a smaller one (X) that needed to be inserted into a larger one (Y) in order to reach food placed some distance from the cage. After the ape learned to do this, Kohler took the smaller stick (X) and replaced it with a stick larger than the first two (Z). Without any hesitation or fumbling, the ape correctly placed stick Y into stick Z to get to the food. Skinner's behavioristic theory would have expected the ape to initially attempt to place Z into Y. Other experiments involved the need to place one or two boxes under a hanging banana in order to reach it. While neither of these experiments was easily solved by the apes, Kohler interpreted their sudden insight into the solution as indicative that the animal could survey the situation, think through the possible success of its behavior, and then test out various solutions.

Language Development—Noam Chomsky

Noam Chomsky (1959) has used research into the development of human language as an argument against the strict empiricist stance of Skinner. Research has shown that children the world over engage in grammatical speech at approximately the same age. This suggests that the environment is not the major factor in human language development. The child-rearing practices of parents (even the presence of mute parents) is not an important factor in language development. The major defining factor in a child's ability to use language is the age at which he interacts with his speaking environment. It appears that children possess a language acquisition device (LAD), or more accurately a grammar acquisition device, that comes into use at about age two. Humans can also speak and understand literally an infinite number of grammatically correct sentences. There is no need to be exposed to and then be reinforced for every correct pattern of words that will ever be used.

All of these ideas seem to point rather strongly to the rationalist and nativist (innate structures) views of language development. Skinner made his empiricist case for language development in *Verbal Behavior* (1957), but when empirical language acquisition is seen in operation, as it is when chimps have been taught to use sign language (object + sign + reinforcement), the tremendous contrast between *how* a child learns language and *how* a chimp does is intensified. This difference strengthens the rationalist's case for human language acquisition.

The Principle of Mass Action—Karl Lashley

Karl Lashley, a student of John Watson, provided evidence that was disconcerting for the staunch associationistic theorists. Lashley (1931) trained animals (generally rats) in running a maze or making a visual discrimination. He would then destroy a part of the animal's cortex, allow it to recover, and then test it to see in what manner its performance had been impaired. The outcome of these experiments was that the amount of cortex destroyed, not its location, determined the deterioration in the animal's behavior. In other words, a given place in the cortex is not the seat of a particular learned performance. (On the basis of this evidence Lashley concluded that the cortex acts as a whole with respect to learning (the principle of mass action), and that lost brain function can be taken over by other areas in the brain (the principle of equipotentiality).

Lashley's work relates to behaviorism in an important way; after his research it was no longer possible to think of the engram, or the physical basis for learning, in terms of synaptic connections in the cortex. Pavlov and Watson's work had stressed the idea that learning was the connection between the incoming sensory stimuli and the outgoing responses. These stimulus-response connections had to be some *place* in the interconnections of neurons mediating the sensory input and motor output. To find out that the synaptic connection is not where the learning "is" was disturbing to the behaviorist to say the least. Lashley's work is not particularly "rationalistic," but it does say that behavior cannot be thought of as simply composed of conditioned stimulus-response relationships, but as much more of a holistic, central process on the part of the brain. Lashley's work forces the search for the mind, learning, personality, emotions, thought, motivation, and so on, away from a strictly behavioristic, peripheral, environmental emphasis, toward the idea that the central processes of the brain are of prime importance in the mental life and activity of the person.

Observational Learning—Albert Bandura

Albert Bandura (1974) expressed his case against the radical behaviorism of psychologists in his presidential address at the 1974 meeting of the American Psychological Association.

> Originally, conditioning was assumed to occur automatically. On closer examination it turned out to be cognitively mediated. (p. 124)

> But external consequences, influential as they often are, are not the sole determinants of human behavior, nor do they operate automatically. (p. 124)

Bandura feels that the consequences of one's actions serve primarily as an information function. By observing the effects of their actions people can discern which behaviors are appropriate in which settings. Reinforcement then changes behavior in humans through the intervening influence of thought. The consequences of our behaviors can also motivate us. Many of the things we do are consciously designed to gain future benefit or to avoid problems. Anticipated consequences are usually more effective in changing our behavior than actual consequences, and thus partial reinforcement is more effective than complete reinforcement.

It is also obvious from Bandura's research that people can learn by observing and not just by experiencing (Bandura, 1971). The human mind's capacity to represent modeled behaviors symbolically enables man to acquire new behavior through observation without reinforced enactment. The observations serve later as a guide for action. Bandura has conducted many experiments on observational learning, particularly with children. In the typical experiment, the subject watches another person perform some action. Later the subject's behavior is tested to see how much of the model's behavior he will demonstrate. Comparison with control group subjects suggests that the learner learns simply by watching the model. Bandura's (1965) now famous "Bozo doll" experiment is illustrative of observational learning. In this experiment children view a film of an adult hitting and kicking a plastic Bozo doll. These children learned aggressive responses through the observation of the film and demonstrated a similar aggressiveness when given an opportunity to play with a Bozo doll.

Skinner's theory may explain how similar behavior that a person has previously learned is being prompted by the prospect of reward. But it cannot explain how a new response is acquired observationally. This learning must be taking place through symbolic processes before any responses have been performed and reinforced. Bandura believes something is going on inside the organism that affects its response to stimuli and influences the value of reinforcers. Furthermore, he looks at the human capacity for thought and language, human learning without reinforcement, and the general planning that guides people's lives rather than specific behavioral objectives as further indications that there is a cognitive dimension behind human behavior.

Stage Theory of Development—Jean Piaget

Jean Piaget, the "giant in the nursery" who died in 1980, contributed an enormous legacy to the rationalist position in psychology. In his stage theory of intellectual development he emphasized that there is a readiness to learn that is provided by the maturation of the child. Piaget's stage theory describes how the primitive thought of infants gradually develops into mature adult thought. This cognitive development of the child depends on both biological maturation and environmental influences. Piaget has described four major stages of development, each of which grows out of the stage preceding it: the sensorimotor period (0–2 years), the preoperational period (2–7 years), the period of concrete operations (7–11 years), and the period of formal operations (from 11 years onward).

In the sensorimotor period the child's intelligence is manifested in his actions as he is interacting with his world by sucking, kicking, hitting, and shaking. Later in this stage the child will develop the concept of object permanence, which has developed when the child begins to reach for an object after it has been hidden from view, having watched it being hidden. At almost two years of age, the child begins to mentally represent the world through images and symbols.

In the preoperational period the child begins to use words to represent things and is developing the concepts of time and number and is learning to put objects in classes. The preoperational mind is still egocentric, meaning the child has difficulty seeing a situation from another's perspective.

In the period of concrete operations, children can perform some new mental operations. Egocentric thought is not as prominent, and simple mathematical operations like adding and multiplying are possible in this period. What is not yet present in the child's mind is the ability to do abstract thinking. The hallmark of development during this stage occurs when the child learns the principle of conservation, the idea that a quantity remains the same in spite of changes in its appearance. The child can recognize that changing the shape of clay, for example, or dividing it into parts, will not change the total amount of clay.

FIGURE 7

The ability to conserve volume involves the ability to recognize that two equal quantities remain equal even if the volume is redistributed.

Finally, in the period of formal operations the child moves from concrete operations to formal, operational thinking. At this level, children begin to solve problems. Hypotheses are formulated and tested, and conclusions are based upon the results. The child's thinking has now become more abstract and logical, like that of an adult. Thus, the development of the cognitive process is complete.

Again, as in the case of language development, it appears as if the environment plays an important but indirect role in the intellectual growth of the child. Differences in parenting or advanced training of the child alter only slightly the structured unfolding of the child's intellectual capabilities. Development rests largely on maturation, although it may be hindered by an unfavorable environment or advanced by a favorable one. Thus, Piaget's theory is a weighty, centralist theory and needs to be dealt with by the peripheral theory of Skinner.

SUMMARY In summary, it can be said that Skinner's view of the mind has not been supported by evidence from the operant conditioning laboratory and runs counter to much psychological data. Skinner sees all aspects of mental life as a product of the environment and physiological states of the body. He has not, however produced experimental evidence of primary and secondary reinforcement that would support a conditioning theory of mental phenomena. Skinner's view of the mind also fails to account adequately for a wide range of impressive psychological data that does not support a strictly empirical view of the mind. The nativist data of Chomsky and Piaget, and the cognitive implications of the research of Bandura, Tolman, and Kohler seem to suggest that while Skinner's behaviorism may explain simple, animal or human behavior, it fails to explain the complexities of human mental life. As Daniel Robinson (1979) put it:

> It is to the credit of Skinner and of those who have adopted his program that we now possess an immense catalogue of experimental findings describing the subtle and durable effects of "reinforcement contingencies". This part of the overall contribution is as impressive as it is unimpeachable, but as Skinner him-

self has moved beyond the data, as he has attempted to include under the umbrella of the law of effect the entire range of human activities, the Skinnerian system has repeatedly foundered and failed. (p. 138)

THE QUESTION OF FREEDOM

6

With the publication of *Beyond Freedom and Dignity* (1971), Skinner's view of human determinism exploded upon the public with its denial of human freedom and suggestions for human engineering. Although determinism has a long history, the prestige of today's science and the popularity of psychology combined with Skinner's literary forcefulness are presenting a strong challenge to the traditional view of human freedom and responsibility. That challenge is the focus of this chapter.

Since some of the greatest minds in history have not resolved the issue of freedom and determinism to everyone's satisfaction, there is no reason to expect that we could do so in a few pages. Consequently we will limit ourselves to an evaluation of Skinner's case for determinism in the light of the data of operant conditioning. We will also look briefly at some of the practical philosophical problems for a deterministic view of human nature.

WHAT DOES SKINNER BELIEVE ABOUT FREEDOM? Skinner's views of human freedom are fairly common knowledge because of *Walden Two* (1948) and *Beyond Freedom and Dignity* (1971). To Skinner the belief in a human agent who is the initiator of his own behaviors is an illusion. He believes that the controlling factor of all human behavior is the environment, or more specifically, the contingencies of reinforcement in that person's past and present environment. Not only outward behavior, but even inner feelings, motivations, reasonings, and rational choices are conditioned products of the environment. In *Beyond Freedom and Dignity* (1971) Skinner wrote:

> What is being abolished is autonomous man—the inner man, the homunculus, the processing demon, the man defended by the literatures of freedom and dignity.
>
> His abolition has long been overdue. Autonomous man is a device used to explain what we cannot explain in any other way. He has been constructed from our ignorance, and as our understanding increases, the very stuff of which he is composed vanishes. Science does not dehumanize man, it dehomunculizes him, and it must do so if it is to prevent the abolition of the human species. To man qua man we readily say good riddance. Only by dispossessing him can we turn to the real causes of human behavior. Only then can we turn from the inferred to the observed, from the miraculous to the natural, from the inaccessible to the manipulable. (p. 191)

The determinism of Skinner leaves one with a different kind of mechanistic man than John Watson's determinism does. Watson's emphasis was on reflex conditioning; it produced a picture of man the robot pacing through the activities of the day with the same reflex action as that of a knee jerk. Skinner's view of emitted behavior, however, leaves a person *feeling* free and *apparently* choosing much of the behavior he will engage in. But in actuality he is just as determined as the reflex man of Watson.

DETERMINISM OR INFLUENCE? It is difficult to imagine any experiment that could be designed to prove the case for determinism (or free will). Would it prove determinism to observe that 100% of the people at a certain beach wear bathing suits? That represents a perfect correlation between an environment and a behavior, but does it mean that those individuals have been determined to wear bathing suits as opposed to having chosen to do so? Does it prove determinism to demonstrate that when a person's arm is twisted he can be made to drink water? Certainly, in my own case, swimming and pain are two examples of what I would describe as strongly compelling stimuli in determining my behavior. But could I ever demonstrate determinism by the mere description of environment and behavior?

It might also be asked whether demonstrating that human behavior *can* be conditioned leads automatically to the conclusion that human behavior *is* so conditioned in real life? Does demonstrating that a person has no apparent control over some extreme stimulus contingencies, mean that in other areas of his life he is also determined? I raise these questions to suggest that Skinner has been less than cautious in using the results of human and animal conditioning experiments to make pronouncements about human determinism. *A careful analysis of the data suggests that influence, not determinism, is a more convincing description of what Skinner has demonstrated.* Human freedom does not mean that a person is not *influenced* by the environment, or that in certain situations he might not be determined by the environment. It simply means that the persons are agents, capable of making choices about what they do.

SECONDARY REINFORCEMENT AND COMPLEX BEHAVIOR

A major feature of Skinner's theorizing is the application of his theory of operant conditioning, which was developed by reasoning from relatively simple animal behavior to extraordinarily complex human actions. He bridges this huge gap by relying heavily upon the concepts of shaping, chaining, and secondary reinforcers we discussed in chapter 3. A complex behavior is supposedly made up of numerous smaller behaviors, and the whole complex function is maintained by a steady supply of secondary reinforcers. Although human behavior is undoubtedly too complex to spot the multitudes of minute conditioning events that shape complex behaviors, if Skinner's view is accurate, some of the more obvious primary and secondary reinforcement contingencies for any behavior ought to be visible.

To demonstrate, let me ask the question, According to operant conditioning theory, why do students attend my classes? Since very little human behavior is in the control of primary reinforcers like food or water, we must look for frequent secondary reinforcers that are maintained by occasional primary reinforcement. My students, then, are not attending class because I distribute candy after every class; there are easier ways to obtain food. They are attending class for what Skinner would consider secondary reinforcement, that is, grades, praise, entertainment, and knowledge.

From what is known of secondary reinforcement in the laboratory, there should be a conditioning history for the development of these reinforcers. Perhaps in my students' earliest school years good grades were rewarded with praise or ice cream, and bad grades resulted in punishment. From animal studies it is clear that secondary reinforcers (e.g., praise, grades) have to be repeatedly paired with other conditioned reinforcers (e.g., money, attention) or with primary reinforcers (e.g., food, water) in order to continue their effectiveness and prevent the extinction of learned behaviors. But my students' class attendance (or any behavior for that matter) does not reveal a maintenance of secondary reinforcers by primary reinforcement. In fact, human secondary reinforcers are extraordinarily strong and resistent to extinction even though possible related primary reinforcers are far removed in time. Human secondary reinforcers, such as conversation, praise, achievement, and others appear to be better explained by Bandura's cognitive factors or Maslow's hierarchy of needs.

Other examples from daily human behavior pose similar difficulties for the determinist who sees behavior as totally controlled by reinforcement. How does operant conditioning theory explain the words a poet chooses when he writes a poem? Can the properties of the present and past environments that are determining the choice of his next word be identified? Furthermore, any stimulus properties found must be shown to be conditioned and unconditioned reinforcers with the same characteristics as those that the theory of operant conditioning would predict. But such contingencies of reinforcement are not apparent in daily human behavior.

"REBEL" BEHAVIOR   When observing human behavior or reflecting on our own, it becomes quite clear that much of the time we resist reinforcement or brave certain punishment in order to engage in certain behaviors. My students have to drag themselves out of bed, face inclement weather, endure uncomfortable desks, and fight off sleep in order to attend my classes. A champion athlete will rise before the sun, endure hours of grueling exercises, and expend much physical and psychological energy on his sport. But what reinforcement causes this behavior? A few tennis players work for cash, Olympic athletes expect gold medals, but most athletes do not win money or gold medals. Weekend joggers and eight-year-old little league baseball players are not paid either.

To say that there is a tremendous physical and psychological exhileration in the expenditure of energy and the excitement of competition ignores the hours of pain and years of grueling practice that must occur before these brief exhilarating moments. In fact, it does not feel exhilarating to get out of bed in the morning. If operant conditioning were accurate in describing human behavior, the world would come to a grinding halt since everyone in it would follow the path of least resistance by remaining in bed for long hours, eating endless meals, and relaxing comfortably all day! Yet much of our behavior apparently rebels against this reinforcing environment. We must rise above our environment to work and play, and this way we build the massive legacy of human achievement throughout the world.

In what other way can the actions of some of the great individuals of history, who have not conformed to the expectations and reinforcement contingencies of their day be explained? Their histories reveal refusals to settle for the easy life, or the safe life, or the accepted, traditional modes of behavior. In what other way can we explain the creative behavior of individuals? Creative behavior involves rebelling against the traditional, accepted, praised, and

FIGURE 8

Many human behaviors result in more pain than pleasure.
This fact is not in line with the operant conditioning theory.

rewarded ways of thinking and doing things. The creative artist, inventor, or scientist may find acceptance later in life or long after he is dead, but this is invariably preceded by years of apparently unreinforced behavior. In addition, what classroom teacher or prison warden has not noticed the "rebel" who does not respond to the rewards and punishment set up for him in a token economy?

Skinner explains all of these examples of rebel behavior by pointing out that it is obvious that for some people the tradiitonal reinforcements or punishments are not reinforcing or punishing. To stay in bed may be reinforcing to you, but not for someone else. To lose your job and be sent to prison may be punishment for you, but not to a Russian dissident. There are other nontraditional stimuli that must be reinforcing their behaviors. This is called the hidden-parameters argument because Skinner is saying that there *must* be reinforcers "hidden" out there in the environment, because he knows his theory is correct! This is a nice try but it fails both logically and scientifically. To begin with, Skinner simply tries to explain away any conceivable evidence against his theory. All that he has to do is to say that there is a reinforcer out there someplace for every complicated human behavior. We just don't know where it is! From this position, Skinner does not *produce* "evidence" for his theory of determinism. He simply claims the reinforcement is out there somewhere because otherwise humans would not be engaging in behaviors that they do. The question is, has careful observation and experimentation revealed such reinforcement systems? The answer is no, this hypothesized "hidden reinforcer" is a product of his theory, not of his experimental evidence.

By the hidden-parameters argument, Skinner is again assuming the very thing that is in question, namely, whether or not human behavior is controlled by the environment. Our objection is that it seems as if much human behavior either goes against the obvious contingencies of reinforcement or braves certain punishment. Skinner's replies that it is clear that since such reinforcements are not reinforcing and such punishments are not punishing, there must be other nontraditional reinforcers. Skinner argues that a person would not be engaging in these behaviors unless they were being reinforced by the environment. But the argument is circular. Is all human behavior controlled by reinforcements from the environment? To argue by using hidden parameters instead of evidence does not answer the question. And thus, the fact remains that much of human behavior stands in apparently clear contradiction of Skinner's view of determinism in man.

THE LOSS OF TRUTH   Although the lack of evidence for Skinner's view is a serious weakness, that is not the only problem. If one accepts Skinner's determinism, certain of its ramifications must also be accepted. Skinner's behaviorism tells us that a person's past and present environment is responsible for all of his behavior. This means that if Skinner encounters a devout Christian or a devout atheist, he would say that their environments had led them to these different ideas and behavior patterns. If a person identifies himself as a Republican as opposed to a Democrat, according to Skinner it is because he has a complex determining background that includes the political preferences of his parents, his yearly income, and his religious preference.

In these examples it is not because of a search for truth that a person ends up with a religious or political preference, but because of environment. *One cannot really know what is true in any area of knowledge.* For example, the reader of this book cannot know whether my evaluation of Skinner's behaviorism is true or not, since it is merely the product of my particular educational and religious background.

Although this inability to discover truth is not troublesome to Skinner, it must at least be pointed out that it applies to his own teachings also. If determinism is true, then every idea that comes from Skinner's mind is a product of his particular environment. If he had experienced a completely different past history, he could now be teaching in defense of human freedom and not against it! Therefore, why should anyone believe what Skinner says about determinism? His has not been an unbiased, scientific search for truth, but behaviors and ideas conditioned by the environment! It is not that truth does not exist or that it is not present in the teachings of people. The problem is that we could never *know* whether we had found truth.

THE LOSS OF RESPONSIBILITY   Another difficulty with Skinner's behaviorism is that its view of responsibility seems unrealistic and unrelated to daily life. The title of Skinner's book, *Beyond Freedom and Dignity*, means that he believes that human freedom does not exist and consequently neither does human dignity as a product of the credit we give individuals for good and distinguished behavior. If Skinner is right, then we cannot hold criminals responsible for their bad behavior, for they have only been conditioned by their environments.

It would be interesting to know what might go on in the mind of Skinner if ever he would be robbed. Like any of us he would probably feel that the criminal should not be robbing him. If the criminal pointed a gun at him, he might say, "Please, don't shoot me!" Such a plea would imply that the criminal had freedom, since Skinner would be holding him responsible for the robbery and asking not to be shot, as if the criminal had a choice in the matter. This example would not be convincing to Skinner because he would say that our thoughts about other's freedoms are simply wrong, his own included. But the point is that all of us (including Skinner) would find it so objectionable to no longer hold anyone responsible for his own behavior that we simply would refuse to live that way. It is difficult to imagine a world in which we would not hold others responsible if they refused to give us our pay check, show up for work on time, stop killing people, and other such things. It is not that the environment doesn't influence what a person does; we would simply find it impossible to shift the entire responsibility for what every person does to the environment.

Skinner, however, does try to be consistent with his deterministic beliefs. In an article entitled, "A Case History in the Scientific Method," Skinner (1961) describes some of his past experiments as a way of showing how he was conditioned to behave by his environment and the animal subjects he used. He also used to chart his cumulative professional behavior in his office just as he did with his animals. Many times in his writings he uses words that refer to himself as having been conditioned by his past. In his autobiography he says that his wife "reinforced" him appropriately when he taught the psychology of literature (Skinner, 1967). When asked why he bothers to write a book if all behavior is determined anyway, he says that to answer that, you have to look into the reinforcement history of a behaviorist!

But in spite of his protests Skinner often continues to use the language of freedom and dignity, almost as if real communication about human beings cannot be carried on without it. In *Beyond Freedom and Dignity* (1971) he seems forced to use language in which he attributes part of the person's behavior to his own initiative:

> When an individual engages in intentional design of a cultural practice. . . . (p. 210)
>
> He is controlled by his environment, but we must remember that it is an environment largely of his own making. (p. 215)
>
> To refuse to control. . . . (p. 5)

Is it not also inconsistent with belief in determinism for Skinner to urge his listening and reading audience to rise up and change the world with behavioral technology? His last sentence in *Beyond Freedom and Dignity* (1971) challenges us, "We have not yet seen what man can make of man" (p. 206). This is paradoxical; how can Skinner put man into the determined, natural order and then ask him to control that order? How can a totally determined organism transcend his environmental determinism to take charge of an environment that totally determines him? Yet Skinner repeatedly suggests that human beings can and should exploit his scientific knowledge of mechanized man in order to raise themselves to new heights of kindness, intelligence, and happiness.

Albert Bandura (1974) has given the same criticism of Skinner's determinism.

> To contend, as environmental determinists often do, that people are controlled by external forces and then to advocate that they redesign their society by applying behavioral technology undermines the basic premise of the argument. If humans were in fact incapable of influencing their own actions, they would describe and predict environmental events but hardly exercise any intentional control over them. (p. 136)

The criticism that Skinner fails to live as he is determined may seem superficial. In fact, when pressed for why he lives with a certain amount of unconscious recognition of his own and other's freedom, Skinner merely has to say, "I am determined to do so." And yet, maybe our behaviors speak more loudly than our words about our beliefs. If a man tells me he does not believe that it is possible to gather any truth from sensory experience, and I later observe him picking a fly out of his hamburger, what am I to conclude? Is he just going through the motions of plucking an imaginary fly out of his imaginary hamburger so that he will not have to imagine eating it? Or do his actions show that no matter what he says he really does trust in what his senses tell him? On the level of daily life, Skinner, too, finds it difficult to live the "truth" he teaches. It seems reasonable to gauge what people really think as much by their behavior as by their theoretical pronouncements!

In summary, readers of Skinner's works ought to give careful consideration to what his work on operant conditioning has and has not demonstrated. Credit needs to be given to Skinner for developing an enormous amount of data that has revealed the important role of the environment on human behavior. When the nature versus nurture question is raised, one can be confident that a strong influence of the environment has been demonstrated. But what has been both demonstrated in the laboratory and observed in the world at large is influence, not determinism. Those who believe in the freedom and dignity of man need not lose confidence because of B. F. Skinner's behaviorism.

THE QUESTION
OF VALUE AND CONTROL

Undoubtedly, one of the **7** major sources of the resistance to Skinner's behaviorism is the public's fear that it *might* work! A popular book, (and movie) *A Clockwork Orange* (1962), helped heighten the public's fear of the power of science. Alex, whose name means "without law," is the lead character in *A Clockwork Orange*. He is a young gang leader who commits one horrible crime after another. Living in a world that contains millions of people like Alex makes normal citizens desperate to accept any psychological solution offered. But the psychoengineering offered in the book seems so repugnant and degrading to those who believe in human freedom and dignity that one is left wondering if it is wrong to apply it, even to a person like Alex.

In great contrast to *A Clockwork Orange,* Skinner's *Walden Two* (1948) tells of a very pleasant community where the measures of control are not visible and where everyone is healthy and happy. Skinner's positive description makes everyone (except philosophers like the book's Professor Castle) desire to move in.

Skinner should be credited for thinking beyond the laboratory to the problems facing the real world. Too often scientists are wrapped up in trivial research that produces dozens of scholarly publications (and perhaps tenure!) but does not relate to the larger world. Not that all science has to be applied, but, without application, science can become a monumental exercise in trivia. In contrast to such irrelevant research, Skinner (1970) dreams of a better world:

> It is hard to imagine a world in which people live together without quarrelling, maintain themselves by producing the food, shelter, and clothing they need, enjoy themselves and contribute to the enjoyment of others in art, music, literature, and games, consume only a reasonable part of the resources of the world and add as little as possible to its pollution, bear no more children than can be raised decently, continue to explore the world around them and discover better ways of dealing with it, and come to know themselves accurately and, therefore, manage themselves effectively. (p. 204)

In order to accomplish all of this, Skinner believes that the principles of operant conditioning need to be applied on a larger scale.

Unfortunately (according to Skinner) the literatures of freedom and dignity and the public's fears of loss of freedom and unscrupulous control are blocking the successful application of this kind of technology. This is one reason why Skinner attacks the writings of C. S. Lewis. Skinner believes he must displace the "unscientific" views of man with his "scientific" one and thus calm the fears of control. He writes (1971):

> It (technology of behavior) will not solve our problems, however, until it replaces traditional prescientific views, and these are strongly entrenched. (p. 25)

In this chapter, we will look at both the possibility of exercising the type of control Skinner advocates and the value questions inherent in this type of behavioral control. We will begin with an examination of the possibility of behavioral control.

THE EFFECTIVENESS OF
BEHAVIORAL TECHNOLOGY

In spite of all of the laboratory success in applying operant conditioning methods to animals, serious questions remain about the feasibility of effectively applying these techniques to a variety of complex human functions, let alone to society at large. The main attempts that have been made are in the area of behavior therapy, and even there, some major limitations have become apparent.

Behavioral therapists' greatest successes have tended to come with individuals suffering from rather specific symptoms of a circumscribed nature. A variety of phobias, for example, have been shown to respond well to behavior therapy (Bandura, Blanchard, and Ritter, 1969; Wolpe, 1963, 1969). Behavioral techniques have also proven effective in weight loss programs (Penick, Filion, Fox and Stunkard, 1971; Stuart, 1971) and in curtailing smoking behavior (McFall, 1970; Nolan, 1968). Some progress has also been demonstrated in the treatment of withdrawn and even autistic children (Louvass, 1967; Schopler, Brehm, Kinsbourne, and Reichler, 1971), unmotivated delinquents (Bandura, 1969; Bednar, Zelhart, Greathouse, and Weinberg, 1970), and chronic schizophrenics (Atthowe & Krasner, 1968; Ayllon and Azrin, 1965). As we move from the more circumscribed symptoms to disturbances of the total personality, however, the effectiveness of behavioral methods to radically alter personality is increasingly called into question.

While behavior therapy has been used to reduce odd behaviors and promote greater cooperation on psychiatric wards, it has not been effective in resolving the confused thinking of psychotics or leading them back to emotional health or maturity. In this regard, behavior therapy for emotional problems might be compared to taking aspirin for a fever. It works, and lesser problems may be resolved, but it may not touch the source of the fever.

Another limitation of behavioral approaches is in getting people to cooperate. In hospital token economies, about 20% of chronic schizophrenics refuse to take part in the token economy and thus fail to emit behaviors that can be reinforced; in prisons, token economies are often resisted by means of organized strikes or sit-ins (Geiser, 1976). It seems that if people know they are being controlled, they resist it. The inherent desire and ability to exercise one's freedom could explain this failure.

Another consistent weakness of token economies is their failure to transfer from the treatment program to the normal living environment. Since the outside environment has a different reinforcement system, the behaviors learned in therapy may not continue in other situations. Consider a prisoner, for example, who has learned to avoid fights in a prison through use of a token economy program. When he is released he may learn that fighting outside the prison produces its own reinforcement. Consequently, unless the larger environment can be controlled, token economies will be of limited value. Such limitations suggest that applying behavioristic technology to the whole of society is impractical no matter how well developed the techniques become. Finley Carpenter (1974) in his book *The Skinner Primer* remarks:

> The main crack in the tight Skinnerian system occurs when Skinner begins to extend his principles to behavior beyond the laboratory. (p. 95)

Operant conditioning can control the behavior of simple organisms because it is carried out in a controlled environment with knowledge of the reinforcement history of the organism, a restricted range of behavior for the organism, and the ability to constantly monitor the organism's behavior and deliver immediate reinforcement. Imagine the difficulty in even the smallest of societies, however, in controlling the minds and behaviors of all of its citizens! How does one arrange reinforcers in order to control the minds of everybody if the controller cannot observe what each person is thinking or feeling at a given moment? We can observe behavior, but one's behavior does not always relate to the thoughts and emotions that have to be shaped and controlled. Even if it were possible to control such inner states, it would be necessary to have a controller for every person. And what controller would be prepared to monitor every behavior and deliver immediate reinforcement?

Walden Two seems to run very smoothly with no apparent controllers only because there are few major behaviors being controlled. Everyone in Walden Two worked, for example, because he received labor credits. But what controlled the hundreds of daily inner behaviors of anger, laziness, jealousy, rebellion, or creativity? These are apparently assumed by Skinner to be smoothly under the control of a society whose members have had all of these inner states conditioned by the proper child development conditioning procedures. But is this possible? Skinner assumes that with a properly controlled upbringing, the whole society would just "naturally" begin to function as a behaviorist would desire, with each person doing and saying the right thing at the right time to reinforce everyone's behavior! There is nothing that has been done in the rat laboratory, the token economy, or communal living situations to suggest that this type of behavioral engineering could ever function in this way.

Our previous discussion about the impossibility of starting or running a Walden-Two society assumes that the behavioristic model of conditioned man may be true. If it is not, and if humans have significant degrees of freedom and self motivation, there is no way Walden Two can work! An operantly-conditioned childhood will not succeed unless the infant is born with a blank slate and does not possess a potential for free choice. One also wonders why Skinner has never attempted to establish his own Walden Two. I do not sense that what is needed is a younger man to pioneer the community, or a few more years to work out the "bugs" in the theory, or an end to the public resistance to the idea of control. A careful analysis of Skinner's view of the person suggests that what is needed is a theory of personality that more accurately fits human nature and the human condition. This is not to say that behaviorism will not find significant success in some types of counseling or limited aspects of social engineering. But Walden Two, like most utopias, will never exist except between the covers of a book and in dreams.

VALUE AND ETHICS   Any discussion about the application of a scientific technology like behaviorism inevitably leads to a discussion about value judgments. Even though we have questioned the feasibility of widespread social engineering, it is interesting to look at some of the problems raised if such control were possible. With a technology in hand, one has to decide what goals it should have and what, if any, boundaries are placed on its use.

Consider the problem facing any counselor. How is he to decide the optimum in human personality or behavior toward which he should guide his clients? A behavior modification expert has to decide whether homosexuality is acceptable or not, and whether or not introverted behavior is acceptable. Today's psychologists generally say that the goal is whatever the client chooses, and that whatever behavior harms the client or others is unacceptable. But these generalizations do not answer the value question. What tells you that the client should decide the goal of therapy, or by what value structure do you decide what is harmful to the client or others? Most counselors make value choices every day without thinking about the source of those values.

The problem of picking values to guide a technology is greatly magnified when we consider the possibility of a behavioral engineer redesigning society. How would the designers of Walden Two choose the kinds of human personalities to develop even if they could exercise such complete control? What thoughts and actions and professions are to be conditioned into the community? And according to what value system did Skinner decide that in Walden Two fashion consciousness was not desirable in women or that early marriage was good. How were any of the thousands of decisions that would shape the future utopia made?

A naturalistic philosophy like Skinner's behaviorism can only arbitrarily decide on a value structure for guidance; it can never insist that any other set of values based on different arbitrary decisions is wrong. This fact shows the relativism in the moral behavior of a secular culture and the paralysis of the "guidance" voice of science. In the famous Rogers-Skinner debate (Rogers and Skinner, 1956) Rogers remarked about the values dilemma of the behavioral engineer, "The value or purpose that gives meaning to a particular scientific endeavor must always lie outside of the endeavor" (p. 16). In other words, even if behavioral technology could produce the massive changes it claims, it could never rightfully say anything about whether the technology should be used or to what ends it should be used.

In order to understand Skinner's answer concerning his source of value in a deterministic system, you must realize that he does not intend to rise out of determinism to "choose" his values. The values he or anyone else may choose are already determined by environment. In a sense Skinner tells his critics not to worry about the choice of values because their environment has already chosen for them.

In Skinner's view, values are automatically produced in the evolving organism. Whatever the organism prefers or finds reinforcing is to be considered valuable because these things have obviously allowed the organism to survive. Since I exist today as opposed to being extinct, my preferences should be considered valid value judgments. For Skinner, the one ultimate value is the survival of the human culture. He writes (1969), "Whether we like it or not, survival is the value by which we shall be judged. The culture which takes its survival into account is most likely to survive" (p. 46).

Looking at Skinner's view that value is that which is reinforcing and aids the survival of man, we can conclude that he believes that whatever is, is good and ought to exist. If a single behavior or an entire culture exists, then it must contain a reinforcing value system and is therefore good. If it is, it is reinforcing; it must be good.

In saying that what is, is good, Skinner seems to be arguing that we need not be completely agnostic about what is ethical and valuable. All that we have to do is to look at our present set of values and observe what appears to be working and what is not. After all, if our culture has survived thus far, it must have much good in its present consensus of value. If it contains too many "bad" behaviors, it will soon die as a culture. But, if someone searches for value by looking at his culture's values to decide what has worked and what has not, he is already using a hidden value system in order to obtain a value system. By what values will I measure what has "worked"?

To assert that anything that exists has value because it has survived means that every existent behavior and every culture is of value; this is highly debatable. Can we look at our own lives or our own culture and make that statement? Philosopher Francis Schaeffer comments appropriately on Skinner's basis for value and ethics in his booklet *Back to Freedom and Dignity* (1972):

> Skinner does not seem to notice that he has gotten himself into a logical box. Ultimately, what he is saying reduces to whatever is is right, and, if whatever is is right, then there is no value over against which one can judge anything as good or bad. If it is, it is good. And if everything that is is good, then any concept of bad is either illogical or trivial. Neither a man like Skinner nor a man like George Wald has any reason why the survival of the race is desirable.
>
> Within the Skinnerian system there are no ethical controls. There is no boundary limit to what can be done by the elite in whose hands control resides. (p. 40)

In considering the practical problem of using Skinner's system of value to guide a future Walden Two, it can be seen that essentially he has no value system to offer. He would have to make decisions as to the goals and values of the culture by trying to discern what would promote the survival of the culture. In the back of his mind, he must already have a hidden set of values to tell him what he means by survival (the survival of physical structures? personality traits? religious ideals?). He must also develop a set of values to weigh the survival of his culture against the survival of other existing, competing cultures, the good of one member of his community rather than another, and the good of the individual versus the good of the community. It hardly seems conceivable that Skinner's basis for value could guide either long range planning or the day to day decisions of Walden Two.

The Question of Control

If there is doubt about the ability of a science to establish guidelines for the use of its technologies, questions and fears are immediately raised about unscrupulous or despotic control measures. But since behavioral technology does not utilize punishment and says that all mental states can be conditioned, Skinner says that fears of *1984* are unfounded. His behavioral technology should produce a world in which everyone would be controlled to feel free, be happy, act kindly, and do all the right things. It would be a control that would never be felt or resisted.

Even though this kind of control would theoretically not "feel bad," it seems to be feared more than the punishing, repressive kind because it involves mind control. At least the slave knows he is a slave and, therefore, has some dignity and freedom in spite of his chains. But in Skinner's world even that freedom would be lost; we would be smiling, happy robots.

In C. S. Lewis' *The Silver Chair* (1953), a good prince, who is a prisoner of the wicked queen, has had his mind altered so that he "willingly" serves her for twenty-three hours a day. But for one hour each day he awakes from his control as from a bad dream and has to be restrained. During his hour of mental freedom he anguishes over what she has done to him. Part of his horror is the realization that at the end of the hour he will again lose the awareness of who he really is and begin again to serve the wicked queen. Not even an hour of freedom would exist in Skinner's system. We fear his kind of control because supposedly we would not know enough to feel unhappy or resent being controlled.

Skinner's answer to all of these fears is a simple one. There is no freedom to lose. You are already being controlled now by your environment! Government, education, parents, and peer groups shape and control your behavior (usually in an unenjoyable, aversive fashion). Do not worry about losing what you do not possess.

But this is not a very comforting answer to those who do believe in freedom and the very real possibility of losing that freedom in a Skinnerian world. When they imagine Skinner's world in operation, they generally see a small group of controllers shaping the lives of the masses. They believe that in order to set up a tightly controlled, deterministic system you have to have your planners and controllers free of the system, to stand outside in order to control its functioning. The planners and controllers then become an elite group that holds the destiny of the masses in their hands. It is this kind of picture that is questioned.

What qualifies these individuals to be controllers? What makes them so good or so knowledgeable that they can successfully do this job? Have they lived such model lives that they can be trusted with such power? Is their knowledge so great that they can shape the destiny of the human race? Do they have all the knowledge of human function and needs as well as the grace to use this knowledge compassionately? Do they have knowledge of all the contingencies of reinforcement affecting a human being and of all possible shaping programs that can work in an entire society? Do our government leaders, or leading scientists, or peers live such model lives and possess such knowledge that we can turn this kind of power over to them? Those who believe in freedom say no.

Skinner's answer to this fear is again very simple and based on his assumption of determinism in man. He says that there would be no elite group of controllers in a future Walden Two. Everyone controls everyone else's behavior right now. The same controllers and controlling situations that exist now would also exist in Walden Two. Government leaders may control the populace, but they would be controlled by voting and other relevant behaviors of the populace. The teacher may control the class, but she is controlled by her students' behaviors. A scientist may be in charge in a laboratory, but his behavior is controlled by the particles or the animals he studies. There is a popular magazine cartoon of two rats in a Skinner Box. Looking up at the researcher, one rat is saying to the other, "Boy, have I got this guy conditioned! Every time I press the bar down, he drops in a piece of food!" To Skinner, this cartoon is true. The scientist may be conditioning the rat, but the rat is likewise conditioning the scientist.

Skinner says we should not fear unscrupulous control in a Walden Two because the controllers would be countercontrolled by the populace. In *Beyond Freedom and Dignity* (1971) Skinner emphasizes this countercontrol. "He is indeed controlled by his environment, but we must remember that it is an environment largely of his own making" (p. 205). This is a way of saying that we are controllers, too, because we are a part of the environment.

It is a legitimate question, though, as to whether everyone has

FIGURE 9

"Boy, have I got this guy conditioned! Every time I press the bar down, he drops in a piece of food." Used by permission of Jester of Columbia University.

the same opportunity to countercontrol. It does not seem that the "followers" could ever be given the necessary tools and the technical know-how to control the "leaders". To Skinner this countercontrol assumes the position of a "law of nature" that operates perfectly without our intervention. But, I can imagine that my screams of pain could keep a bully from breaking my arm, but not keep him from bending the arm just so far. Of what consolation is my countercontrolling scream? It is hard to imagine that his muscles and my screams are equivalent control stimuli.

For many reasons then, if it were possible to control a society, we should be concerned about the application of behavioral technology. If freedom really exists, Skinner's technology would have no guarantees of ethical restraint and guidance. An elite group would have to be set up outside of the controlled system. Controllers would share the very faults they wish to cure us of. Countercontrol would be a myth. Skinner, who does not believe in freedom, would not have to worry about any of these objections. For this reason, his writings have not been reassuring to the reading public. Given his assumptions, he does not have to come up with ethical plans or built-in restraints against unscrupulous controllers. His ideas are shielded by a deterministic box of his own construction.

It should be said that the mere existence of a technology does not justify its application. Even if someone could apply Skinner's technology to society, the tremendous doubts about the deterministic model that underlies behavioral engineering indicate that it would be applied without adequate safeguards and without the needed countercontrol. There is also a danger that human freedom could be retarded by massive doses of extrinsic reinforcement. There is sufficient evidence to suggest that intensive extrinsic reinforcement tends to turn play into work, that is, what you used to do because of intrinsic motivation (play), you now will only do for extrinsic reinforcement (work). Perhaps the direction that psychology should pursue is to develop the internal motivation of individuals and teach them how to use extrinsic reinforcers, as opposed to a massive attempt to control the whole of society with a Walden Two system.

SKINNER'S ANSWERS TO HIS CRITICS

The last four chapters have **8** discussed the serious limitations of Skinner's under- standing of human nature. Skinner is not oblivious to these criticisms; he responds by saying that a fuller understanding of his laboratory findings will answer the doubts of his more philosophically minded critics. Skinner's critics (Wheeler, 1973) contend, however, that the issues are not the kind that can be resolved by pointing to scientific data; they insist that Skinner uses assumptions for facts and then makes grandiose pronouncements about the nature of man from selective data.

A look at Skinner's interactions with his critics suggests that very little real communication is going on between them. Reading the Rogers and Skinner (1956) debate, for example, makes it clear that while each presents his arguments well, they fail to win be- cause they are speaking from such different underlying assump- tions. Although Skinner's answers are reasonable within his radical behavioristic view of things, they really do not resolve the prob- lems Rogers raises from his phenomenological perspective. The best way to acquaint the reader with the problems of the dialogue however, is to let Skinner speak for himself. Skinner's responses to the following objections should help clarify his stand and demonstrate some of the problems of communication between Skinner and his critics.

SKINNER SAYS THAT HUMANS ARE MECHANIZED ROBOTS Skinner denies that his behaviorism describes human beings as automatons. Although this might accurately describe the determinism of the classical conditioning theory of Watson in which stimuli *elicit* responses in a reflex fashion, Skinner does not view his theory this way. He writes:

> But stimuli do not *elicit* operant responses; they simply modify the probability that responses will be emitted. They do so because of the contingencies of reinforcement in which they have played a part, and they may act in combination with other conditions, possibly but not necessarily to the point at which a response occurs. This is a far different role from that of the eliciting stimulus in a reflex. (p. 245)

In other words, Skinner says we should not confuse his theory with a theory that builds all human behavior out of reflexes. Skinner agrees that most human behavior is of the operant kind, that is, behaviors emitted by the organism at "will" and not elicited by some stimulus. But emitted behaviors, according to Skinner, are no less determined than elicited behaviors. They just appear to be emerging by the choice of the organism. In actuality, they are being controlled by the reinforcing environment.

Since the feelings and thoughts of a person are also controlled by the environment, the person may have all the experiences of feeling free choices, motivation behind behavior, and creative thoughts, but in actuality these feelings of freedom are illusions. Therefore, human behavior has none of the appearances or feelings of automated behavior. But, to Skinner we are nonetheless controlled. If we were to visit a future Walden Two, its inhabitants would not appear in any way mechanized or controlled in their behavior. According to Skinner they would feel exactly as people always have, except perhaps a little happier.

SKINNER'S THEORIES DEHUMANIZE MAN AND DESTROY HIS FREEDOM

Supposedly what is meant by this criticism is that Skinner's theories have not recognized the whole of human nature, and his behavioral technology would destroy man as man along with human freedom. Skinner's answer to this objection is that you cannot destroy something that is not there in the first place. Human nature and human freedom simply do not exist. Our only evidence that they exist is the presence of feelings of freedom and creative thought and language. But these are only products of the environment. Behaviorism does not take these away; it merely describes them for what they really are. Skinner (1974) writes:

> A science of behavior has been said to dehumanize man because it is reductionistic. It is said to deal with one kind of fact as if it were a different kind—as is done, for example, by physiological psychology. But behaviorism does not move from one dimensional system to another. It simply provides an alternative account of the same facts. It does not *reduce* feelings to bodily states; it simply argues that bodily states are and always have been what are felt. (p. 265)

A major criticism concerns the weight Skinner seems to put on the scientific analysis of thought and feeling. He is claiming that his science has successfully explained where thoughts, intentions, and emotions come from as well as their relationship to the environment. But this is simply not the case. Skinner has extrapolated his findings on animals and simple behaviors and applied them to the complex world of a person's inner experience. In very vague and sketchy descriptions he "guesses" how the environment might produce everything from self-awareness to the great literature of the world. If Skinner is wrong, and human nature and freedom are real (as evidence leads us to suspect), then his behaviorism is reductionistic and leaves us with a significantly dehumanized description of man.

SKINNER DENIES
THE EXISTENCE OF THE MIND

Skinner does not deny the existence of an inner realm of thought and emotions. What he does deny is the common interpretation of these feelings as coming from some mysterious entity called the mind or soul or self or any other name we wish to give it. Skinner's radical behaviorism does not deny mental states like methodological behaviorism or logical positivism, which refuse to consider them. He says that what is felt, or introspectively observed is not some nonphysical world of consciousness, mind, or mental life. It is only a product of the body's interaction with the environment. Skinner comments on this (1974):

> In the sense in which we say that a person is conscious of his surroundings, he is conscious of states or events in his body; he is under their control as stimuli. . . . A person becomes conscious in a different sense when a verbal community arranges contingencies under which he not only sees an object but sees that he is seeing it. In this special sense, consciousness or awareness is a social product. . . . No special kind of mind stuff is assumed. A physical world generates both physical action and the physical conditions within the body to which a person responds when a verbal community arranges the necessary contingencies. (pp. 241–42)

Once again Skinner's view of the mind is highly speculative and will find little acceptance without the support of further research. Skinner's ideas have done little to discredit the more rationalistic approaches to explaining the mind, which show evidence of a much smaller role for the environment in the development and functioning of the human mind.

SKINNER CONSIDERS
CONCEPTS OF VALUE AND ETHICS
IRRELEVANT

Skinner does not consider values and moral behavior irrelevant in a practical sense; he certainly has moral concern and makes value decisions in every-day life. He also believes that counseling and behavioral engineering require a set of values and an explicit ethical system. He feels, however, that these values are not derived from a "god out there" or from some built-in motivation toward the good. What we call good or valuable is a product of the reinforcing environment. Ultimately, we call those actions good that are reinforcing to us. A good personality trait is one that is reinforcing to you. A valuable person to have in the community is one who contributes to the survival of the community. Skinner (1974) says:

> the behavior we call moral or just is a product of special kinds of social contingencies arranged by governments, religions, economic systems, and ethical groups. We need to analyze those contingencies if we are to build a world in which people behave morally and justly, and a first step in that direction is to dismiss morality and justice as personal possessions. (pp. 268–69)

Skinner (1974) feels that the admirable moral qualities in us are a product of the countercontrol of others.

> When we ask why a person is benevolent, devoted, compassionate, or public spirited, we find ourselves examining the effect his behavior has on others. . . . The consequences responsible for benevolent, devoted, compassionate, or public-spirited behavior are forms of countercontrol, and when they are lacking, these much-admired features of behavior are lacking. (p. 210)

Skinner's answer tells us why many people behave in good and moral ways, but it does not really tell us how we can know what is good and moral behavior. To say that good and moral behavior is that which is reinforcing describes not just good but all repetitive behavior. According to Skinner, if it was not reinforcing, the behavior would not exist. But how does he know it is wrong for a man in the street to steal a woman's purse? If the man keeps doing it, we must assume that he finds it reinforcing. To say that good behavior is that which is reinforced leads to saying that purse snatching in many instances may be good. Skinner does argue that such acts are not ultimately reinforcing (if the man gets caught and goes to jail). But that doesn't answer the question as to why purse snatching or any immoral act does not become extinct on the earth because of lack of ultimate reinforcement. The history of our planet should tell us that bad behaviors have not decreased at all in the last few thousand years!

While Skinner does not consider value and ethics irrelevant, he lacks an adequate foundation for discussing or making moral decisions. What if the victim of the purse snatcher wonders whether it is moral for her to shoot the thief? What would Skinner say to her about the morality of her act? Is it even possible to provide her with information about the ultimate consequences of her act on the survival of the community?

TRUTH IS UNDISCOVERABLE GIVEN SKINNER'S DETERMINISM If everything a person says has been conditioned by his background, then we cannot know that what he says is true. If he had a different background, then he would be teaching some other position. If we apply Skinner's logic to his own teachings, for example, we could ask why he (or anyone else for that matter) should believe that his teachings on radical behaviorism are true. Ultimately, we could not say they were true but rather that we have been conditioned to believe they are true!

Skinner deals with this criticism in *Verbal Behavior* (1957) by pointing out all the complicated research supporting his theories. But Skinner's choosing to run certain experiments in certain ways and with certain interpretations of the data are also determined. Why did he choose to perform his research on animals, for example? Did that not shape his findings? Consequently, how can he know his research points toward truth in understanding humans?

Skinner (1957) comments on this:

> But have I told him the truth: Who can say? A science of verbal behavior probably makes no provision for truth or certainty (though we cannot even be certain of that). (p. 456)

He says, speaking of scientific knowledge (Skinner, 1974),

> There is a special sense in which it could be 'true' if it yields the most effective action possible. . . . a proposition is 'true' to the extent that with its help the listener responds effectively to the situation it describes. (p. 259)

It can be seen by these quotes that Skinner avoids discussing truth as absolute. The only definition for truth that determinism leaves is "that which is effective," or "that which works." But this definition is meaningless unless we can know what "effective" actions are. How can we know what an effective action is unless we already have some truth about effective actions?

Skinner cannot satisfactorily answer the problem of the loss of truth because no answer is possible unless we assume that the universe and all its inhabitants just naturally evolve toward a truth that works. This still does not tell us if our knowledge at any particular moment is true until long after we raise the question, and so it leaves us suspended over the gaping chasm of skepticism.

SKINNER'S BEHAVIORAL ENGINEERING OPENS US UP TO UNSCRUPULOUS CONTROL

To Skinner, questions such as, Who will control? or Might not evil men use Skinner's powerful technology? are irrelevant questions. In the deterministic system everyone is already controlled by something in the environment even if he calls it self control. The only change in a behavioral technology is to arrange the contingencies of control, rather than let them operate randomly. This means that even the controller is controlled by his environment, which includes those he supposedly controls. That such countercontrol exists is Skinner's reassuring answer to us.

> When a person changes his physical or social environment "intentionally"—that is, in order to change human behavior, possibly including his own—he plays two roles; one as a controller, as the designer of a controlling culture, and another as the controlled, as the product of a culture. (1971, p. 197)
> To say that all control is manipulative and hence wrong is to overlook important uses in education, psychotherapy, government, and elsewhere. A proposal to terminate behavioral research or to sequester its results on the grounds that they can be used by despots and tyrants would be a disastrous mistake, because it would undermine all the important contributions of the

culture and interfere with the counter-controlling measures which keep aversive and exploitative control within bounds. (1974, p. 268)

Skinner's statements about countercontrol are only meaningful and reassuring if determinism is true and everyone is controlled by evenly balanced contingencies in the environment. However, that is assuming that life is like a poker game in which every player continually has an equal number of poker chips with which to bet. But, as we glance around the "table" of life, that does not appear to be the case. Some individuals in this life, for whatever reason (chance, talent, environment, et al.), do seem to hold more control over the major reinforcements and punishments than others. Countercontrol capabilities may exist somewhere in the environment to control the despot, like Hitler, but millions of his citizens did not seem to have a handle on how to countercontrol. To say that Hitler was countercontrolled by the advancing Allied troops ignores the fact that he was more in control of German and Jewish citizens than they were of him. If men are not determined, then we ought to worry about unscrupulous control, because controllers could resist the influences we create in their environments and *choose* instead to exercise aversive power.

SKINNER'S RESEARCH WITH ANIMALS AND SIMPLE BEHAVIORS RELATES VERY LITTLE TO THE COMPLEXITY OF HUMAN NATURE Skinner is quick to point out that this objection is assuming that human behavior is somehow different from animal behaviors or simple responses, which is a question for science to answer. In responding to this objection Skinner (1953) says:

> To insist upon this discontinuity at the beginning of a scientific investigation is to beg the question. Human behavior is distinguished by its complexity, its variety, and its greater accomplishments, but the basic processes are not therefore necessarily different. Science advances from the simple to the complex; it is constantly concerned with whether the processes and laws

discovered at one stage are adequate for the next. It would be rash to assert at this point that there is no essential difference between human behavior and the behavior of lower species; but until an attempt has been made to deal with both in the same terms, it would be equally rash to assert that there is. (p. 38)

More recently Skinner (1974) writes that enough experimentation has been done to warrant holding to these initial extrapolations from animal behavior that he has applied to complex human behavior. He says, "Enough has been done to suggest that the same basic processes occur in both animals and men." (p. 250)

Skinner has made a good point that if science, especially the science of human behavior, is to be successful, it must begin with the simple before analyzing the complex. And the use of animal subjects has a long and accepted history in psychology. The problem with this answer, however, is that one should not begin and end with the simple experiment. There have been operant conditioning experiments run on human beings, even in complex environments. But there have been too few of them and the connections between the results in the Skinner Box and the results in human experimentation have been poorly made, if at all.

Human experimentation that has not controlled for the subject-experimenter interactions, the past history of the subject, and the cognitive "behavior" of the subject cannot be safely assumed to demonstrate the truth of Skinner's theories. Human experiments may be difficult to run and control, but Skinner has never seriously attempted to demonstrate his theories in complex human behaviors. In fact, Skinner's major views on human nature were written during the height of his animal experimentation and before much human experimentation had even been attempted.

Also, it is not begging the question to be open to the possibility that humans are qualitatively different from animals. Since Skinner's assumptions on the identical behavioral bases for both human and animal behaviors seem as of yet undemonstrated by scientific experimentation, are they not "begging the question" just as much as the views of human nature that posit some radical differences between human and animal nature?

SKINNER DOES NOT LIVE AS IF DETERMINISM WERE TRUE. WHY DOES HE USE MENTALISTIC TERMS? WHY DOES HE WRITE A BOOK?

Skinner's basic answer to these questions is that whatever he does, he has been determined to do by his environment. If we wonder why he does something, he suggests that we study his environmental history. If we wonder why a man who believes that we are determined would ever write a book urging us to *choose* to do something, he responds that he is determined to write such a book (Skinner, 1974).

> According to the traditional definitions of self-control, happiness, decision, responsibility, and urging, the behaviorist is indeed inconsistent, but according to his own definitions he is not; and when the latter are understood, objections of this sort lose their force. (p. 272)

To the question, "Why does Skinner even bother to write a book?" he responds (1974):

> To answer that question we should have to go into the history of the behaviorist. Nothing he says about human behavior seriously changes the effect of that history. His research has not altered his concern for his fellow men or his belief in the relevance of a science or technology of behavior. (pp. 272–73)

This answer may be correct within Skinner's deterministic system, but it is hardly a satisfying answer to those raising the objection. It is not clear what is going through the mind of Skinner as he writes his books. Does he consciously think of his book as a stimulus that will in someway change human operant behavior? Or do his actions reveal a belief that people are free and can change their behavior if urged to do so?

To the specific objection that he uses mentalistic language in the very books that condemn mentalistic constructs, he writes (1974):

> I have used technical terms in making a technical point. I have preferred a technical term elsewhere when it could be used at no great cost. Rather than say that our problem is "to create a concern for the future," I have preferred to say that it is "to induce

people to act with respect to a future." I prefer the expression "It occurred to me." But elsewhere I have freely used the lay vocabulary while accepting the responsibility of providing a technical translation upon demand. There is no other way if a book of this kind is to be brief and readable. (pp. 271–72)

SKINNER IGNORES ANY PSYCHOLOGY THAT DOES NOT AGREE WITH HIS SYSTEM

Skinner does not respond favorably to other areas of psychology, primarily because he rejects any attempt to theorize about physical or mental constructs in order to account for human behavior. He says in an interview with *Psychology Today* (Hall, 1967):

> I think the main objection to behaviorism is that people are in love with the mental apparatus. If you say that doesn't really exist, that it's a fiction and let's get back to the facts, then they have to give up their first love. . . . This Freudian business is dying out, anyway. As for the cognitive seed, that never was anything; they are not getting anywhere; and the operant people are. . . . When all their mythical machinery finally grinds to a halt and is laid aside, discarded, then we will see what is remembered fifty or a hundred years from now . . . you can't get results by sitting around and theorizing about the inner world of the disturbed. (p. 109)

Skinner's rejection of most areas of psychology illustrates the academic isolation of his radical behaviorism. His system is so restrictive that it can benefit from no other kind of data or theories in psychology. The problem is not just that Skinner neglects cognitive and physiological data, but that his behaviorism offers no sufficient method to study such ideas in order to reject them.

SKINNER'S BEHAVIORISM REPRESENTS SCIENTISM, NOT SCIENCE

Skinner insists that his behaviorism has been more scientific than almost any area of psychology. He feels that his emphasis on the investigation of basic processes with careful attention to the design and control of experiments is what science is all about. He says (1974):

> Behaviorists are sometimes accused of idolatry; they are said to worship science and to borrow the trappings of science simply in order to look scientific. . . . But it is hard to find any sign of this in the history of the experimental analysis of behavior. Early studies used simple equipment, and the data were reported as simply as possible. The underlying assumption that behavior was orderly rather than capricious could scarcely be said to have been adopted for honorific purposes. To establish the dimensions of behavior and related variables, to insist upon prediction and control, to use mathematics where quantification permitted— these were essential steps rather than window dressing. (p. 256)

While it is true that Skinner should not be accused of operating unscientifically in the laboratory, that is not true about the many statements of "fact" that he bases on assumptions about the nature of reality, humankind, and knowledge rather than upon experimentation. It is in these areas that Skinner's philosophical assumptions influence his statements and are offered as the findings of science rather than as one narrow philosophical perspective—here he can perhaps rightly be accused of scientism.

SUMMARY In general it can be seen that there is not a lot of effective communication going on between Skinner and his critics. The communication that exists leaves neither side impressed by the other's arguments. This is largely due to the fact that Skinner and his critics are arguing from radically different starting assumptions about reality and human nature. Skinner's seeming disinterest in the kind of questions that philosophers raise is not due to an ignorance on his part of the philosophical arguments, but to his belief in the truth of his radical behaviorism. In the same way, some hostility to Skinner's ideas probably arises because his critics are inclined to reject all of his work because of his unacceptable philosophical framework. More meaningful dialogue would ensue if Skinner's critics attempted to understand his scientific findings and ideas in the context of their own philosophical assumptions about reality and man. In the next chapter I will attempt to suggest some of the directions this effort could take for those interested in relating Skinner's work to historical Christian thought.

A CHRISTIAN RESPONSE

Our analysis of B. F. Skinner's **9** research and theoretical labor has shown that his strong points lie in his scientific methodology and laboratory data. Skinner has made immense contributions to psychology with his operant-conditioning paradigm and its numerous applications to animal and human learning. He has explored and quantified some of the ways we are affected by our environment; he has gone a long way toward explaining how this process works—at least in animal behavior and some simple human activities. The application of behavioristic principles to the field of clinical psychology by those who had been influenced by Skinner is also providing a technology to deal with a variety of psychological disturbances. The impact of Skinner's theory of human and animal behavior has without a doubt changed the entire field of psychology. Few other theorists in the one-hundred-year history of psychology have contributed so much.

On the other hand, Skinner's journeys into the realm of philosophical speculation on human nature seem to go far beyond what his data will support. His dogmatic dependence upon a single, empirical method for knowing about human nature has narrowed his scope of understanding of the human personality on issues like language, freedom, dignity, and ethics. It has also left him opposing many respected views on human nature. In chapters 4–8, we looked at some of the major conflicts between Skinner's assumptions on human freedom and competing views, and also at some of the serious gaps in Skinner's theorizing. However, we have not yet directly addressed the question of the compatibility of Skinner's views on human nature with those of Christianity. In this chapter we will look at some of these key areas and attempt to see precisely what areas of compatibility and conflict exist. To do this, we will look at various aspects of Skinner's theories that the Bible also speaks to. Specifically, we will look at the biblical view of human nature, human freedom, and the source of value and ethics. As a foundation for this, we must also take a brief look at the biblical view of reality, including the reality of God and the nature of His revelation.

In attempting to set forth some fundamental features of the Bible's views of reality and human nature, I am not attempting to erect a biblical psychology or to give detailed statements on the human personality. The Bible, in general, limits its teachings on human nature to brief but far-reaching descriptions concerning the origin and destiny of man and the relationship of man to God and other men. It is debatable whether a complete "biblical psychology" can be constructed from such content. While the Bible does not exhaust the subject of human nature, and while it does not give detailed or specific descriptions of how the personality functions, it does provide some very clear parameters and definitive statements that enable us to evaluate at least the broadest and most fundamental concepts of theorists like Skinner.

THE NATURE AND KNOWLEDGE OF REALITY In an earlier chapter, we critiqued Skinner's strictly materialistic and naturalistic assumptions about the nature of reality. Since he sees the entire world (including humanity) as composed of only matter and operating by laws of cause and effect alone, he rules out the existence of any reality other than material realities and denies the validity of any methods of knowing except pure empiricism. He writes (Skinner, 1971, 1974):

> The picture which emerges from a scientific analysis is not of a body with a person inside, but of a body which *is* a person in the sense that it displays a complex repertoire of behavior. (p. 190) A person is not an originating agent; he is a locus, a point at which many genetic and environmental conditions come together in a joint effect. (p. 185)

In this chapter, we will examine Skinner's views of the nature of reality and the nature of persons to discover how well they fit with biblical revelation.

The Bible stands dramatically apart from the naturalistic, materialistic pronouncements of our age to assert that God exists and that He is the source of all that is. The Bible opens with, "In the beginning God created" (Gen. 1:1). John tells us, "In the beginning was the Word, and the Word was with God, and the Word was God" (John 1:1). God was there before there was material reality. According to Scripture, the Creator is not an impersonal force, but a personal being who has revealed Himself to humanity. The existence of a personal, creative, communicating God does not permit us to understand life solely in natural and material terms. Although a restricted, materialistic view might be helpful for the limited purpose of scientific predictability, we cannot expect to fully understand any part of the universe apart from both God's creative purposes and continuing activity. Hebrews 1:3 aptly tells us that He sustains "all things by his powerful word." This is apparently a continuing, active sustaining of the universe. The Bible does not present God as the deist's absent God or a God who is there but is in no way involved with the natural order. Donald MacKay (1974) writes:

> I think, the key to the whole problem of the relation of science to the Christian faith, is that God, and God's activity, come in not as extras here and there, but everywhere. . . . If the divine activity means anything, then *all* the events of what we call the physical world are dependent on that activity. (p. 57)

When the scientist discovers the laws of nature, he is not discovering exceptions or alternatives to God's activity; he is simply describing that activity in its physical manifestations. The Christian view of God, in fact, does not allow us to separate the activities of God from the activities of nature. Consequently, the Christian has no quarrel with Skinner's data. Skinner has uncovered some of God's laws governing certain animal and human behaviors. The problem arises only when Skinner generalizes from his data and makes broad assumptions about the nature of reality that are unsupportable by data and in conflict with biblical revelation. At the very moment Skinner is attacking the "nonscientific" views and assumptions of theorists who disagree with him he is operating on his own unprovable assumptions. As E. J. Carnell (1948) put it:

> The mistake of the modern man is that he pronounces the benediction when the scientist has spoken, not realizing that there are yet superhypotheses which must be made before even the subordinate laws of science are significant. (p. 94)
>
> The enigmatic situation in the modern world is that the scientist rejects the Christian world-view because it involves certain non-empirical metaphysical hypotheses, while assuming for himself a truckload, each of which goes as much beyond sensory observation as does the Christian's postulate of the God Who has revealed Himself in Scripture. The Christian questions the sport of this game. Fair rules in the contest of hypothesis-making ought to dictate that the winner be he who can produce the best set of assumptions to account for the totality of reality. If the Christian is disqualified from the arena by rules which his opponent makes, it is evident that the game has been 'fixed.' Good sportsmanship, to say nothing of common sense, requires that in a contest, all participants be given the same advantages as well as the same handicaps. Without these conditions there is no sport. (p. 94–95)

Rather than yielding to Skinner's attempt to baptize his theoretical assumptions about reality in the waters of "science," the Christian needs to consider the foundation of these assumptions and compare them to biblical ones. The Bible affirms that we can gain knowledge through the revelation of God as well as through naturalistic methods and that the combination presents a more adequate picture of the nature of reality. The historical position of the church is that God has revealed truth about Himself and His creation in two ways. General revelation comprises the truths that God reveals through nature and history that can be grasped by the human intellect because as bearers of the image of God we are intelligent, rational beings. These truths can be grasped by scientific investigation, observation, logic and so on; Skinner's empirical findings would be considered part of general revelation.

Special revelation, on the other hand, includes truth communicated through the Bible and the person of Jesus Christ. In the study of human nature, we need special revelation because empirical investigation in this field is limited and biased by false assumptions. There are many truths about human nature that cannot be assessed by scientific methods or deduced by our logic. Such things as man's immaterial nature (if it exists!), life after death, purpose in life, and ethical absolutes cannot be investigated adequately through strict empiricism or rationalism. The special revelation of Scripture treats many of these questions that are not within the range of empirical science and, consequently, adds immeasurably to our understanding of human nature. Both science, which studies the universe God created (general revelation), and the data of Scripture (special revelation) provide a view of the nature of reality and a broader access to truth—especially about the human personality.

Psychologists who like Skinner have no belief in a Creator have a limited source for fully understanding personality and recognizing the distinctions between mankind and the animal world. They reject the humanity's distinctive creation in the image of God.

Skinner apparently holds tenaciously to a view that makes man a biological machine and it is difficult for him to see personal man as the exception in a nonpersonal, material universe. That would limit the applicability of his research and consequently humanity's efforts to control its own destiny. Skinner sees his rejection of man as a personal, self-directing species as freeing us for future growth and development. In reality it does precisely the opposite. By so limiting his focus on sources of knowledge to empirical methods, Skinner actually binds the study of the person to a narrow and restrictive band of functions, and leaves untouched the essential uniqueness of humanity. In "freeing" the science of psychology to use only empirical methods for the study of observable behavior he would actually bind us from the study of the areas of personality that are most distinctively human!

The Bible, as revelation from God, is a source that makes it possible for Christians to study more successfully what has to be the most complicated subject matter in the universe—human nature. It has been said that the mysteries of the brain alone rival the complexity of any other phenomenon in the universe. Indeed, in order to learn more about the intricacies of our whole beings, we will need a method of knowing that is capable of seeing beyond the limited range of empiricism—one that can give us a complete picture of man. Only from the perspective of the Creator Himself can the deepest questions in human life be answered.

THE QUESTION OF HUMAN NATURE Skinner's detailed studies on operant conditioning have emphasized how closely human behavior is tied to reinforcements in the environment; they have helped to demonstrate that the human mind is not an independent entity, but is influenced, sometimes rather strongly, by the bodily states of a person. With this, the Christian has no problem. Skinner's radical behaviorism, however, and his reductionism teach that thinking, willing, and feeling are nothing more than physiology interacting with the environment. His view runs counter to the Christian perspective of the person as being endowed with an immaterial essence that relates to, but is not controlled by, the material body.

It is difficult to summarize the biblical view of human nature since it would undoubtedly fill many volumes. There are a few features, however, of the biblical doctrine of man that are especially relevant to Skinner's view of human nature. The impression the Bible gives us concerning humanity is in conflict with Skinner's behaviorism in that man has central position in the whole of reality. Humanity is the peak of creation and the object of divine love. Our supreme value is that we are children of God who can possess a dynamic, intimate relationship with the Creator. The teaching and actions of Jesus emphasize the worth of man; the Sabbath was made for man, not man for the Sabbath (Mark 10:31). Man is more valuable than the animals (Matt. 10:31, Luke 12:7; Matt. 12:12), and man's eternal soul is of more worth than anything in this world.

Another prominent feature of the biblical view of human nature is that man is not an isolated, self-explained being. In fact, Scripture emphasizes that man cannot be understood or explained aside from his relationship to God. G. C. Berkhouwer (1962) explains:

> We cannot understand "man" apart from his relation to God. Man would then be, from a scriptural viewpoint, nothing but an abstraction, and if we seek to define man merely in terms of various qualities and abilities, we are not giving a biblical picture of man. (p. 93)

This means that while we may learn much about man with empirical methods, those methods can never disclose the total reality of man's essence. Man's whole being is dominated by the fact that he was created to enter into, and live out a loving, dependent, and obedient relationship with God. Jeremiah 10:23 tells us that a man's life is not his own. The mystery of personality is bound up with dependence on and interaction with the Creator.

Since mankind was created to know God and to commune with Him, it stands to reason that God would make human nature capable of a personal relationship with Himself. There are limitations to bodily existence (Gen. 2:7–3:19), but the Bible also teaches that human beings are a special creation made similar to God. While much debate surrounds the precise meaning of the image of God in man, we can safely assume that this image and likeness relates to the personality of man. As persons we are agents of our own behavior. We are creative, rational, moral, and social beings. And most importantly, we stand apart from the animals in our capacity for a deep and intimate relationship with God.

The Bible also emphasizes the essential unity of human nature. Genesis 2:7 describes human life as the unity of the physical and spiritual. "And the LORD God formed man from the dust of the ground and breathed into his nostrils the breath of life, and man became a living being." This holistic view of human nature is important when evaluating Skinner's behaviorism. Human nature, while intricately physical, is not merely biological. On the other hand, in emphasizing the existence of personality, we must not divorce mental life from the body and thereby ignore the environmental influences upon human nature.

Another relevant aspect of the biblical view of human nature is the fall into sin. According to Scripture, the first human pair rebelled against God and threw the entire human race into alienation from the Creator and from each other. Although this fall did not destroy the image of God in man it did seriously distort it. Man lost communion with God and the inclination to God's will; there was no possibility for self-recovery. According to Scripture, all of humanity's problems—physical, social, and psychological—can ultimately be traced to this spiritual alienation and the excessive self-centeredness caused by the Fall.

The five elements of the biblical view of humanity we have just surveyed (the central position of man in God's created order, the impossibility of understanding man apart from his relationship with his creator, the essential differentiation of man from the animal kingdom, the holistic view of the nature of persons, and humanity's sinfulness) are in agreement with many psychological observations of humanity. Man towers above the animal world in his reason, morality, emotional expression, culture building, and person-social relationships. In contrast, Skinner attempts to attribute the entire range of humanity's ability, potential, and creative genius to simply the physical and environmental realms. His view does not accord with these broad, biblical observations. The Christian view, which sees our uniqueness as originating from and relating to the God of the universe, seems much more consistent with the amazing achievements and potentials so apparent in human nature. Although relating humanity's genius to the creative activity of God is not provable by the methods of science, it is no less provable than Skinner's naturalistic and materialistic assumptions, and it appears to be at least as capable (if not more so) of explaining the unique phenomena of human nature.

In addition to fitting more naturally with our observations of the fundamental differences between humans and animals, the biblical view of human nature, which stresses humanity's relationship to God, provides a firm basis for identity and self-worth. Skinner's behaviorism can only provide a fragile foundation for self-esteem based on arbitrary pronouncements of self-worth in a cold universe in contrast to the living, dynamic foundation for self-esteem that grows out of viewing man as a creation of the living God!

The biblical emphasis on the unity of man's nature is also in agreement with neurophysiological studies, which show a very close relationship between brain activity and human functioning. If man is a unified being, we cannot understand human nature as simply a summation of various parts. We must be alert to a dynamic interaction of the whole person with the environment.

The Christian view of the Fall (and potential redemption) allows us to look more deeply at the source of humanity's emotional, behavioral, and social problems than if we attended simply to environmental factors. Although a discussion of the causes of psychological maladjustment is beyond the scope of this book, Skinner's concept of the person as a blank slate that is shaped toward goodness or badness by the environment simply does not account for the perversity of human nature as well as the biblical view. While recognizing these environmental influences, the Christian view also attends to the basic propensity of humans to respond in selfish and self-defeating ways. The Christian concept of sin provides this balancing frame of reference.

THE QUESTION OF FREEDOM The determinism of human nature as taught by Skinner springs ultimately from his denial of the uniqueness of the human personality. The biblical concept of human freedom flows logically from the view of humanity as a bearer of the image of God. It seems clear that the Bible teaches the essential freedom of human nature. The Old and New Testaments are filled with God's requirements for human behavior. God holds human beings responsible for their actions and expects them to correct sinful behavior. God also clearly desires that His love toward humanity will be returned. In fact, the whole drama of sin and evil, beginning in the garden of Eden and continuing until this day, implies that something has gone wrong in God's universe. God created human beings with the freedom to act counter to His will.

While Skinner's research has uncovered a basic lawfulness relating human and animal behavior to the environment, these factors do not destroy freedom any more than our basic sinfulness destroys our ability to be responsible. If we use the term *influence* instead of *determinism*, Skinner's contributions (and those of many other behavioral psychologists) can be placed in a more realistic perspective. The Bible makes it clear that human beings influence each other (Prov. 22:6), and the view of an "influencing" environment also allows for the existence of freedom (freedom does not have to mean choices without influence). There can be little doubt that everything we are, is at least in part a product of the environment in which we exist, but this does not destroy human freedom, it simply balances it and puts it in perspective. We live in a complex universe ordered by God in which we have the power to make willful choices that impact both our lives and the lives of others. There is a balance between individual freedom to choose (which we all have) and the influences of others upon our choices.

This biblical view of man's freedom does not assert that free actions are capricious, uncaused happenings, that are unrelated to either one's past history or environmental influences. It suggests instead that free behavior is ultimately caused by the person himself in the context of these other variables. These other variables are a necessary part of the explanation of human behavior since human nature is not separate from the natural order. Such variables, however, are not a sufficient explanation. Evans (1977) speaks about freedom of man within the natural order.

> He becomes what he becomes in the context of these social roles which tremendously limit and weight his options as an agent. Nevertheless, as a rational, responsible agent, he is not merely formed by these social relationships; he acts and by acting helps to form these roles in turn. He is not only constituted by these

relationships; he himself consitutes them. He plays a role in continuing them, modifying them for better or worse, enhancing or degrading their quality and character (p. 145).

The importance of a belief in the freedom of human nature cannot be overemphasized when it comes to using psychology to help solve humanities' personal and social problems. In our design of counseling methods or social programs, believing in human freedom forces us to draw upon the powerful resources of the individual for change (these resources that remain of limited interest to the radical behaviorist). Our belief in human freedom does not deny the influence of the environment on man, but because we believe in freedom we can strive to help a person gain control over his environment. Believing in both human freedom and the strong influences of the environment allows us to retain a view of human responsibility and dignity and at the same time not lose our compassion for those who have been tremendously handicapped by severe environmental circumstances and therefore used less of the potential freedom.

THE QUESTION OF VALUE AND CONTROL One cannot read *Walden Two*, Skinner's utopian novel, without being impressed by his desire to apply his theory to the severe problems faced by the world. Skinner has emphasized what we all should agree to—that human problems today are almost out of control and something needs to be done to help people lead productive, happy lives. Skinner is also optimistic enough to believe that our problems can be solved. As we saw in Chapter 7, however, even if Skinner's methodology could be applied in the optimistic manner *Walden Two* envisions, it would fail to provide any meaningful direction and source of value for the changes taking place. Thus, even its potential value for change in the culture becomes immediately suspect.

In contrast to Skinner's utopia, the Christian has a solid basis for assigning worth to a particular behavior or direction in science because the Bible contains both ethical absolutes and general principles that can guide behavior. The Christian ethic, rather than being the result of arbitrary human decisions, is anchored firmly in the unchanging nature of a God of perfect love and justice. This does not mean that the Christian ethic is based upon the arbitrary will of a supreme being; its basis is the unchanging character of God. Christian theologians Geisler and Feinberg (1980) for example, assert, "If God is all-good and all-knowing as the Christian believes, then He and He alone is in the best position to declare what is valuable and what is not valuable for finite creatures" (p. 367).

The Christian ethic is superior to Skinner's natural ethic because it has its basis in the unchanging character of God. Skinner can only point to what men seem to be doing successfully and claim that this is a "natural law" in their behavior. Actually, what men *believe* ought to be done or how they would *like* to be treated is frequently closer to the natural law in man than is his behavior! With God as the source of direction the Christian has a perfect and loving center of reference whereas Skinner can only rely on the natural inclinations of imperfect men as the source of guidance and value.

The Christian view of change in society also offers a superior motivation than Skinner's reinforcement theory. Since man is a free person, he is challenged by God to do right and love his neighbor because God has commanded it. Furthermore, he is assured continually in the Bible (Pss. 1, 19, 119; Prov. 1–9) that the doing of right will result in blessings. The Christian has hope for a better world, not because his environment will change, but because he has experienced a spiritual rebirth that deeply impacts his basic self-centered propensity. In relationship with God the believer not only knows the good, but has a new motivation to pursue it.

CONCLUSION   In conclusion, it can be seen that biblical revelation is compatible with the data Skinner has gathered and that the data is consistent with an ordered universe created by God. Skinner's findings are a part of our understanding of God's general revelation, and as such are an important part of our understanding of human nature. This same biblical revelation,

BEHAVIORISM IN THE LIGHT OF SCRIPTURE ■ 117

however, is opposed to Skinner's total determinism, narrow empiricism, and naturalistically-based value system. As Christians we should feel free to utilize the findings of Skinner's science in a range of clinical applications. We should not delude ourselves, however, into thinking that his learning paradigm is a fully complete or accurate presentation of the dynamic operations of personality. As Jeeves (1976) put it:

> I must distinguish carefully between Skinner's scientific contribution and his speculative writings. It is in the latter that he freely imports his own values, beliefs, hopes and fears, but this importation should not detract from the importance of the former. (p. 61)
>
> So long as Skinner's model is evaluated on its merits as a contribution to our techniques for shaping and maintaining behavior there is not conflict with Christian beliefs. Conflicts arise when unjustified extrapolations are made, such as that, because aspects of animal and human behavior can be manipulated using their techniques man is therefore 'nothing but' a stimulus-response machine. (p. 62)

As should be apparent from the relative lack of emphasis on the specific clinical applications of Skinner's behaviorism, our analysis of Skinner was not designed primarily to answer questions about the use of behavior modification techniques for weight control, reducing smoking, or stimulating more assertive behavior. Given the Christian understanding of general revelation and the fact that all truth is God's truth, we should not hesitate to utilize workable principles that are consistent with biblical revelation. Our goal in this volume has been to challenge some of Skinner's assumptions; this is part of a larger issue that is signaled by the tendency of some scientists to deny the unique personhood of human beings.

It is perhaps strange that Skinner and other scientists who attack the concept of personhood trace their academic roots back to the age of humanism. Then, as now, it was man in all his glory who sent noble reason around the globe to search out and conquer all the mysteries of nature and lay them at humanity's feet. Then came the day when many of these mysteries of nature were unveiled and man was left with nothing more to conquer except his reason and himself. Having finally conquered these he joined the ignoble ranks of molecule and rat. The optimistic search for truth ended with a loss of truth; exalted man ended up in a Skinnerian box of his own construction!

And yet it is not so strange. Without a larger source for understanding man than nature, a piece of nature he must be. Let us visit briefly with C. S. Lewis (1947) on this concluding thought.

> From this point of view the conquest of Nature appears in a new light. We reduce things to mere Nature *in order that* we may "conquer" them. We are always conquering Nature, because "Nature" is the name for what we have, to some extent, conquered. The price of conquest is to treat a thing as mere Nature. Every conquest over Nature increases her domain. The stars do not become Nature till we can weigh and measure them; the soul does not become Nature till we can psychoanalyze her. The wresting of powers *from* Nature is also the surrendering of things *to* Nature. As long as this process stops short of the final stage we may well hold that the gain outweighs the loss. But as soon as we take the final step of reducing our own species to the level of mere Nature, the whole process is stultified, for this time the being who stood to gain and the being who has been sacrificed are one and the same. . . . (pp. 82–84)

But surely it is not yet too late to argue for a view of humankind that befits its magnificent nature, which at times manifests itself in ways that can easily be understood according to simple laws of learning, and at other times manifests itself in complex ways that defy these naturalistic observations!

REFERENCE LIST

Atthowe, J. M., Jr., and Krasner, L. Preliminary report on the application of contingent reinforcement procedures (token economy) on a "chronic" psychiatric ward. *Journal of Abnormal Psychology,* 1968, *73,* 37–43.

Ayllon, T. and Azrin, N. H. The measurement and reinforcement of behavior of psychotics. *Journal of Experimental Analysis of Behavior.* 1965, *8,* 357–384.

Bandura, A. *Principles of behavior modification.* New York: Holt, Rinehart, and Winston, 1969.

Bandura, A. *Social learning theory.* New York: General Learning Press, 1971.

Bednar, R. L., Zelhart, P. F., Greathouse, L., and Weinberg, S. Operant conditioning principles in the treatment of learning and behavior problems with delinquent boys. *Journal of Counseling Psychology,* 1970, *16*(6), 492–497.

Boring, E. When is human behavior predetermined? *Scientific Monthly,* 1957, *84,*(4), 189–196.

Breland, K. And Breland, M. The misbehavior of organisms. *American Psychologist,* 1916, *61,* 681–684.

Burgess, A. *A clockwork orange.* New York: Ballantine Books, 1962.

Carnell, E. J. *An introduction to Christian apologetics.* Grand Rapids: Eerdmans, 1948.

Carpenter, F. *The Skinner primer.* New York: The Free Press, 1974.

Carter, J. and Narramore, B. *The integration of psychology and theology.* Grand Rapids: Zondervan, 1979.

Chomsky, N. Review of *Verbal behavior* by B. F. Skinner. *Language,* 1959, *35*(1), 26–58.

Cosgrove, M. *Psychology gone awry.* Grand Rapids: Zondervan, 1979.

119

Ferster, C. and Skinner, B. F. *Schedules of reinforcement.* New York: Appleton-Century-Crofts, 1957.

Freedman, P. E., Cohen, M., and Hennessy, J. Learning theory: Two trials and tribulations. *American Psychologist,* 1974, *29*(3), 204–206.

Geiser, R. *Behavior modification and the managed society.* Boston: Beacon Press, 1976.

Hall, M. An interview with "Mr. Behaviorist" B. F. Skinner, *Psychology Today,* September, 1967, 21–23 and 68–71.

Hilgard, E. and Bower, G. *Theories of learning* (4th ed.). Englewood Cliff's, N.J.: Prentice-Hall, 1975.

Jeeves, M. *Psychology and Christianity: The view both ways.* Downers Grove, IL: InterVarsity Press, 1976.

Kohler, W. *The mentality of apes.* (Translated by E. Winter). New York: Harcourt, Brace and World, 1925.

Kuhn, T. *The structure of scientific revolutions.* Chicago: The University of Chicago Press, 1962.

Lashley, K. Mass action in cerebral function, *Science,* 1931, *73,* 245–254.

Lewis, C. S. *That hideous strength.* New York: Macmillan, 1946.

Lewis, C. S. *The silver chair.* New York: Macmillan, 1953.

Louvass, O. I. Behavior therapy approach to treating childhood schizophrenia. J. Hill (ed.), *Minnesota Symposium on Child Development.* Minneapolis: University of Minnesota Press, 1967.

Mackay, D. *The clockwork image.* Downers Grove, IL: InterVarsity Press, 1974.

McConnell, J. Learning theory, in *Introductory Psychology Through Science Fiction* (2nd ed.), Katz, H., Greenberg, M., and Warrick, P., eds. Chicago: Rand McNally, 1977, 264–276.

McFall, R. M. Effects of self-monitoring on normal smoking behavior. *Journal of Consulting and Clinical Psychology,* 1970, *35,* 135–142.

Myers, D. *The human puzzle.* New York: Harper and Row, 1978.

Nolan, J. D. Self-control procedures in the modification of smoking behavior. *Journal of Consulting and Clinical Psychology, 1968, 32,* 92–93.

Pavlov, I. *Conditioned reflexes.* London: Oxford, 1927.

Penick, S. B., Filion, R., Fox, S., and Stunkard, A. J. Behavior modification in the treatment of obesity. *Psychosomatic Medicine,* 1971, *33,* 49–55.

Robinson, D. *Systems of modern psychology.* New York: Columbia University Press, 1979.

Rogers, C., and Skinner, B. F. Some issues concerning the control of human behavior, *Science,* 1956, *124,* 1057–1066.

Russell, B. *Philosophy.* New York: Norton, 1925.

Schacter, S., and Singer, J. Cognitive, social and physiological determinants of emotional state, *Psychological Review,* 1962, *69,* 379–399.

Schaeffer, F. *Back to freedom and dignity.* Downers Grove, IL: InterVarsity Press, 1972.

Schopler, E., Brehm, S. H., Kinsbourne, M., and Reichler. Effect of treatment structure on development in autistic children. *Archives of General Psychiatry,* 1971, *24* (5), 415–421.

Skinner, B. F. *The behavior of organisms.* New York: Appleton-Century-Crofts, 1938.

Skinner, B.F. Baby in a box, *Ladies Home Journal,* October 1945. Also in Skinner, F. *Cumulative record* (Enlarged ed.). New York: Appleton-Century-Crofts, 1961, 419–426.

Skinner, B. F. *Walden Two.* New York: Macmillan, 1948, 1976. Quotes from 1976 edition.

Skinner, B. F. *Science and human behavior.* New York: Macmillan, 1953.

Skinner, B. F. A case history in the scientific method, *American Psychologist,* 1956, *11,* 221–233. Also in Skinner, B. F. *Cumulative record* (Enlarged ed.). New York: Appleton-Century-Crofts, 1961, 76–100.

Skinner, B. F. Pigeons in a pelican, originally an APA paper in Cincinnati, September, 1959. Also in Skinner, B. F. *Cumulative record* (Enlarged ed.) New York: Appleton-Century-Crofts, 1961, 426.10–426.18.

Skinner, B. F. *Verbal behavior.* New York: Appleton-Century-Crofts, 1957.

Skinner, B. F. Cumulative record (Enlarged edition). New York: Appleton-Century-Crofts, 1961.

Skinner, B.F. Behaviorism at fifty, *Science,* 1962, 140, 941–948.

Skinner, B. F. B. F. Skinner in *A History of Psychology in Autobiography,* Vol. 5, Boring, E. and Lindsey, G. (eds.) New York: Appleton-Century-Crofts, 1967, 385–413.

Skinner, B. F. *The technology of teaching.* New York: Appleton-Century-Crofts, 1968.

Skinner, B. F. *Beyond freedom and dignity.* New York: Knopf, 1971. Quotations from New York: Bantam Books, 1972.

Skinner, B.F. Answers for my critics, in *Beyond the punitive society,* Wheeler, H. (ed.). San Francisco: W. H. Freeman, 1973, 256–266.

Skinner, B. F. *About behaviorism.* New York: Knopf, 1974. Quotations from New York: Vintage Books, 1976.

Skinner, B. F. *Reflections on behaviorism and society*. Englewood Cliffs, N.J.: Prentice-Hall, 1978.
Stuart, R. B. A three-dimensional program for the treatment of obesity. *Behavior Research and Therapy*, 1971, *9*, 177–186.

Tolman, E. C. Cognitive maps in rats and man, *Psychological Review*, 1948, *55*, 189–208.
Tolman, E. C., and Honzik, C. H. Introduction and removal of reward and more performance in rats. *University of California Publications in Psychology*, 1930, *4*, 257–75.
Trueblood, E. *Philosophy of religion*. Grand Rapids: Baker, 1973.

Watson, J. *Behaviorism*. New York: People's Institute Publishing Co., 1924–25.
Wheeler, H. (ed.). *Beyond the punitive society*. San Francisco: W. H. Freeman, 1973.
Wolpe, J. Quantitative relationships in the systematic desensitization of phobias. *American Journal of Psychiatry*, 1963, *119*, 1062.
Wolpe, J. *The practice of behavior therapy*. New York: Pergamon, 1969.

ANNOTATED BIBLIOGRAPHY

Bandura, A., *Principles of behavior modification,* New York, Holt, Rinehart and Winston, 1969.

This book, written by one of the major figures in the field, provides extensive treatment of all the different techniques used in behavior therapy.

Bandura, A., Behavior theory and the models of man, *American Psychologist,* 1974, *29,* 859–869.

This APA presidential address of 1974 gives a critical look at behavior theory from a "cognitive" behaviorist.

Bufford, R., *The human reflex: behavioral psychology in biblical perspective,* San Francisco: Harper and Row, 1981.

This is the second in the Harper/CAPS series on Christian perspectives on counseling and the behavioral sciences. Bufford doesn't argue for behavior theory itself, but that the Bible supports the ethical use of reinforcement techniques.

Burgess, A., *A clockwork orange,* New York: W. W. Norton, 1963.

This popular novel is a fictional demonstration of how conditioning and human engineering might work in the real world. It provokes a lot of thought no matter what one feels about Skinner's behaviorism.

Carpenter, F., *The Skinner primer,* New York: The Free Press, 1974.

This is one of the better introductions to Skinner's behaviorism and some of the issues involved. It gives a fair presentation of Skinner's views alongside of a critique of his ideas of freedom.

Chomsky, N., Review of *Verbal behavior* by B. F. Skinner, *Language,* 1959, *35*(1), 26–58.

A now-famous critical look at Skinner's views on language from one of the leading scholars in the field.

Epstein, R. (ed.), *Notebooks, B. F. Skinner,* Englewood Cliffs, N.J., 1980.

This is a rare personal glimpse of Skinner through many of his informal notes on psychology, philosophy, education, language, love, politics, religion, children, history, truth, and more.

Geiser, R., *Behavior modification, and the managed society,* Boston: Beacon Press, 1976.

This book explores the successes and failures of behavior modification and analyzes the conditions under which it does or does not work. He feels that behavior modification has a limited ability to accomplish social change.

Guttman, N. On Skinner and Hull: a reminiscence and projection, *American Psychologist,* 1977, *32,* 321–328.

This article gives a good succinct analysis of Skinner's influence.

Honig, W., and Staddon, E. (eds.), *Handbook of operant behavior,* Englewood Cliffs, N.J.: Prentice-Hall, 1977.

This book reviews research in operant psychology, both basic and applied. It is one of the most comprehensive sources now available and is recommended for serious students.

Lewis, C. S., *The abolition of man,* New York: Macmillan, 1947.

This is a modern classic that describes the abolition of human nature by naturalistic thinking. It is this powerful book that Skinner attacks in *Beyond freedom and dignity.*

Machan, T., *The pseudo-science of B. F. Skinner,* New Rochelle, N.Y.: Arlington House Publishers, 1974.

In this work a trained philosopher gives a response to Skinner's view of man and society and offers an alternative that upholds individual dignity. He demonstrates that Skinner has strayed from hard science in the lab into the world of social philosophy.

Mackay, D., *The clockwork image,* Downers Grove, IL.: InterVarsity, 1974.

This is a book by a respected Christian who is a specialist in brain physiology. He examines the Christian view of freedom and dignity of man and its relation to the scientific enterprise.

Rachlin, H., *Behavior and learning,* San Francisco: W. H. Freeman, 1976.
This is a good general textbook on behavioristic learning theory by one of psychology's most productive researchers.

Rogers, C., and Skinner, B. F., Some issues concerning the control of human behavior, *Science,* 1956, *124,* 1057–1066.
This is the classic debate between the leaders of their respective schools of thought. Positions are well stated without any overly destructive criticism.

Schaeffer, F., *Back to freedom and dignity,* Downers Grove, IL: InterVarsity, 1972.
A short book by a popular philosopher-theologian. He attacks the deterministic views on human nature in modern biology and Skinner's psychology.

Skinner, B.F., *The behavior of organisms,* New York: Appleton-Century-Crofts, 1938.
This is Skinner's classic, first book: he first outlined his theory of learning in this book.

Skinner, B.F., B. F. Skinner, in Boring, E., and Lindsey, G. (eds.) *A history of psychology in autobiography,* vol. 5, New York: Appleton-Century-Crofts, 1967, 385–413.
Skinner's brief autobiography.

Skinner, B. F., *Beyond freedom and dignity,* New York: Knopf, 1971.
This is one of the more explosive books of our time. In it Skinner presents in a more popular way his argument against the literatures of freedom and dignity, and outlines his theory and its application to society.

Skinner, B. F., *About behaviorism,* New York: Knopf, 1974.
From an extensive set of notes written after the publication of *Beyond freedom and dignity* Skinner wrote answers to the critics of his ideas. It is highly readable and can even serve as an introduction to his basic ideas.

Skinner, B. F., *Particulars of my life,* New York: McGraw-Hill, 1976.
In this book the account of Skinner's early years is greatly amplified.

Skinner, B. F., *The shaping of a behaviorist:* Part Two of an Autobiography, New York: Knopf, 1979.
Skinner continues his autobiography in this volume.

Stolz, S., and associates, *Ethical issues in behavior modification*. San Francisco: Jossey-Bass Publishers, 1978.

In 1974 the APA formed a commission to examine and clarify the issues involved in influencing and changing human behavior and to provide recommendations concerning the use and misuse of behavior modification. This book with a foreword by Albert Bandura reports on the results of that commission. It describes and evaluates the variations in practice at a variety of settings where behavior modification is applied.

Wheeler, H., (ed.), *Beyond the punitive society,* San Francisco: W. H. Freeman, 1973.

This is the publication of a conference of thinkers assembled to explore the implications of operant conditioning. Among those submitting papers to the conference were Arnold Toynbee, Arthur R. Jensen, Karl Pribram, Alex Comfort, and B. F. Skinner himself.

Wolpe, J., *Practice of behavior therapy,* New York: Pergamon Press, 1967.

This is a complete description of behavior therapy by one of the noted authorities.